TAKE A TEA TOWEL

16 BEAUTIFUL PROJECTS FOR YOUR HOME

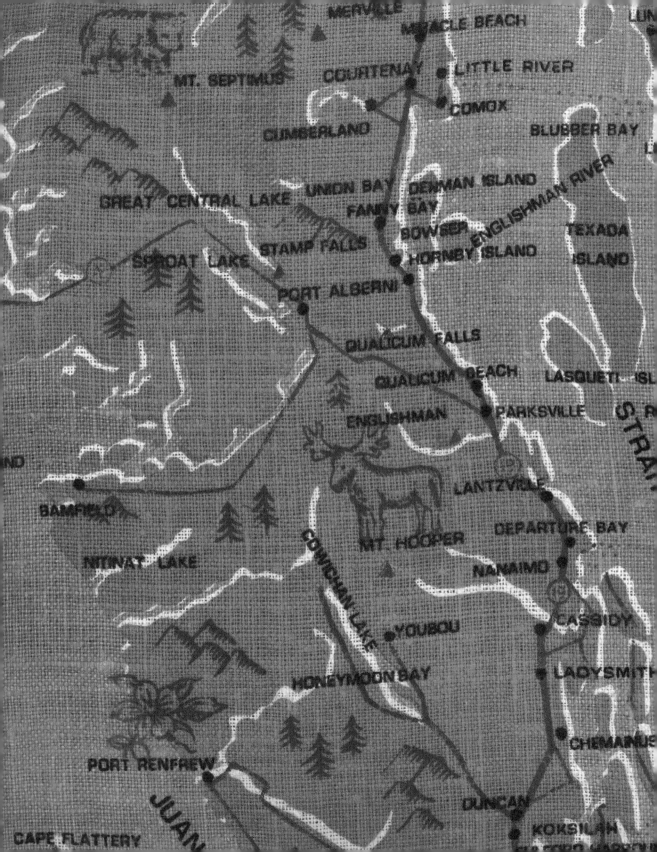

TAKE A TEA TOWEL

16 BEAUTIFUL PROJECTS FOR YOUR HOME

Jemima Schlee

THE GUILD OF MASTER CRAFTSMAN PUBLICATIONS

First published 2015 by
Guild of Master Craftsman Publications Ltd
Castle Place, 166 High Street, Lewes,
East Sussex BN7 1XU

Text © Jemima Schlee, 2015

Copyright in the Work © GMC Publications Ltd, 2015

ISBN 978 1 86108 790 4

Publisher Jonathan Bailey
Production Manager Jim Bulley
Senior Project Editor Virginia Brehaut
Editor Nicola Hodgson
Managing Art Editor Gilda Pacitti
Photographer Holly Jolliffe
Cover Photography Andrew Perris
Step Photography Jemima Schlee

Colour origination by GMC Reprographics
Printed and bound in China

For Harrison and Martha

Contents

Knitting-needle Roll p.40

Coat-hanger Cover p.58

String Holder p.36

Sewing-machine Cover p.32

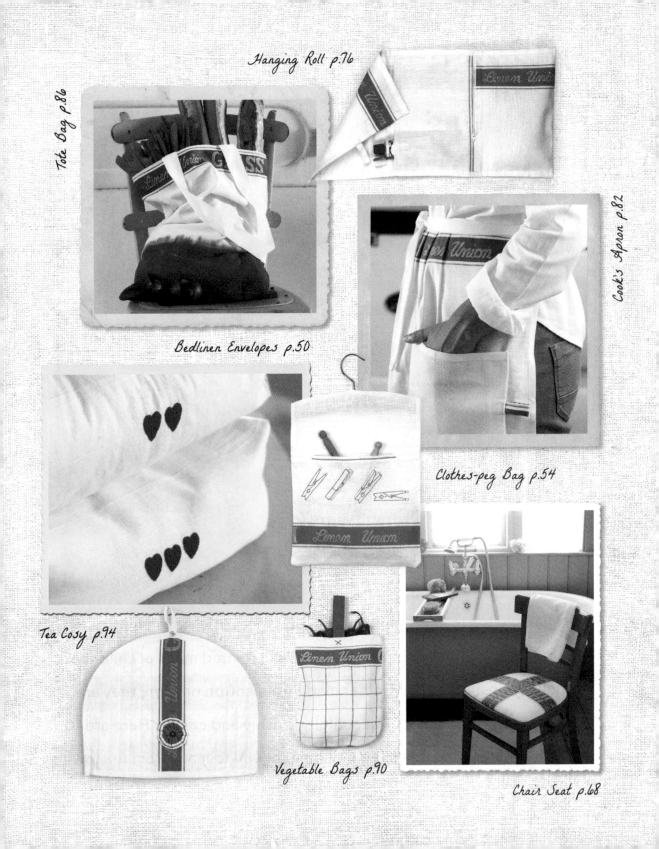

Hanging Roll p.76

Tote Bag p.86

Cook's Apron p.82

Bedlinen Envelopes p.50

Clothes-peg Bag p.54

Tea Cosy p.94

Vegetable Bags p.90

Chair Seat p.68

Don't just dry the dishes with it – take a tea towel and transform an everyday essential into a stylish, original item for your home.

INTRODUCTION

The humble tea towel can be decorated with classic woven gingham or stripes, bright French jacquard or nostalgic printed maps of childhood holiday destinations. Whether made from cotton or linen, they are hard-wearing and launder beautifully, freshly and crisply. Here are 16 practical and timeless items for the home for you to make from tea towels.

TEXTILES MADE FROM LINEN date from as far back as 8000 BCE. In Ancient Egypt linen, symbolizing purity and light, was used to wrap mummies. For centuries, it was considered a sacred cloth and even used as a form of currency. The expense of its production meant it was worn mainly by the wealthier classes and by priests.

Today linen is used to make bed sheets, towels, tablecloths, napkins and clothing. Linen fabric feels cool to the touch and is very durable and strong. Made from flax, linen increases by about one-fifth in strength when wet. It is resistant to moths and gradually becomes softer the more it is washed.

There is a long history of linen production in Ireland and I have used the classic Irish linen glass cloth for the projects in this book. The nostalgic, striped cloths are simple, practical and timeless, sitting comfortably in any interior. I have made use of their bold, coloured edging stripes in my designs.

Any cloth in linen, cotton or a linen-cotton mix, and of roughly the same dimensions of 20 x 30in (50 x 76cm), can be substituted to make your project more personal. Check the sizing in the individual project supplies lists: generally the projects will not suffer from being a little larger or smaller, as long as you have the confidence to make the adjustments.

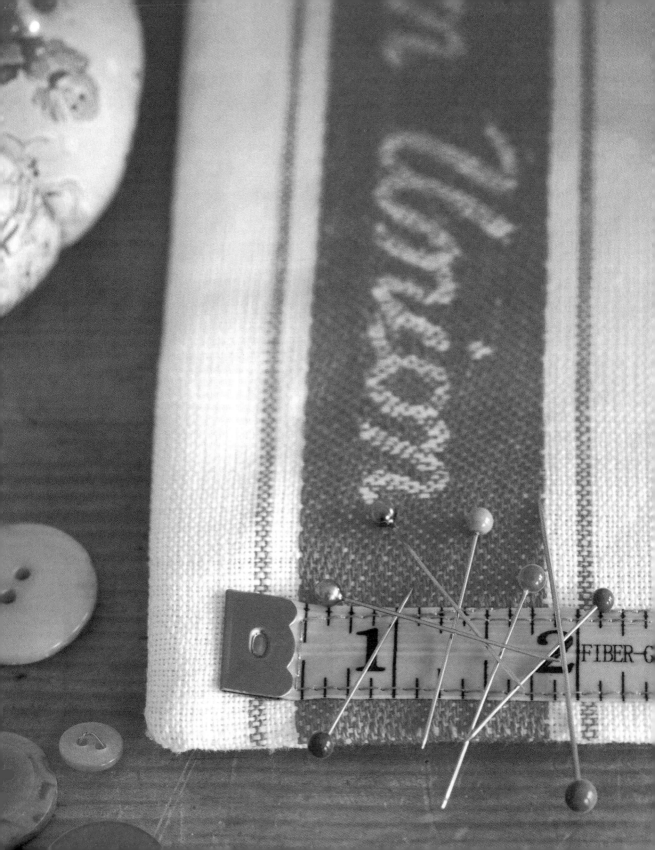

Opposite: Sewing-machine Mat **page 28**
This page: Sewing-machine Cover **page 32**

This page: String Holder **page 36**
Opposite: Knitting-needle Roll **page 40**

This page: Linen Bags **page** 46
Opposite: Bedlinen Envelopes **page** 50

Opposite: Clothes-peg
Bag **page 54**
This page: Coat-hanger
Cover **page 58**

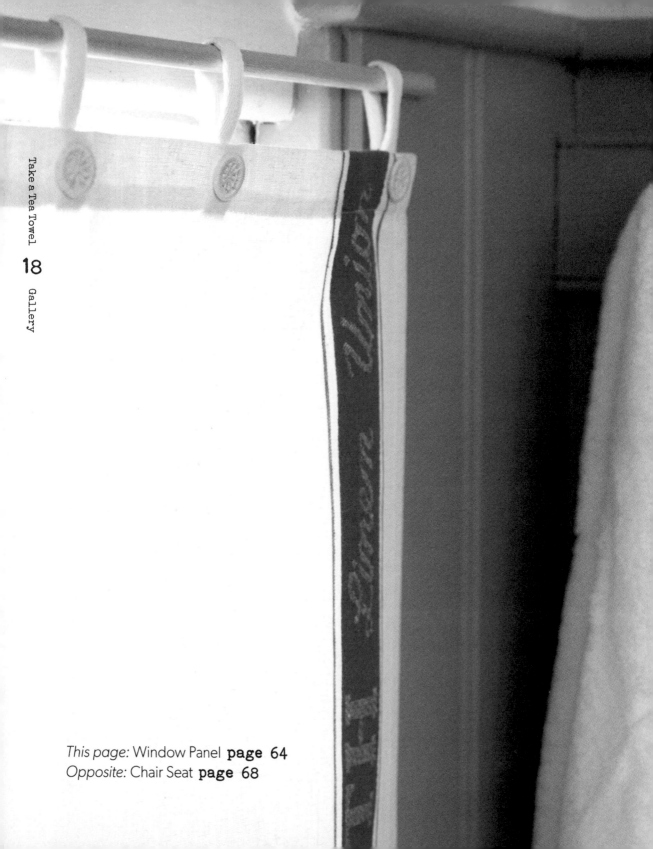

This page: Window Panel **page** 64
Opposite: Chair Seat **page** 68

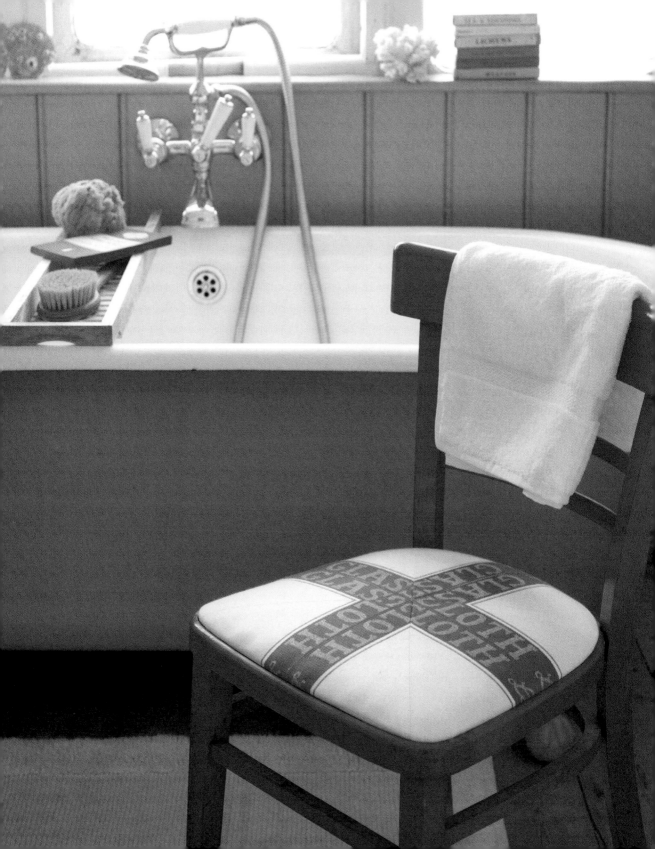

This page: Wash Bag **page 72**
Opposite: Hanging Roll **page 76**

Linen

GLA

Opposite: Cook's Apron **page 82**
This page: Tote Bag **page 86**

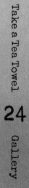

This page: Vegetable Bags **page** 90
Opposite: Tea Cosy **page** 94

THE WORKROOM

This simple little mat does more than just protect your worktable.
It is padded and quilted, with the practical addition of tape measure
edges for checking your hems and seams, plus secreted magnets
to corral your sewing pins while you work.

SEWING-MACHINE MAT

Supplies:

- [ ] 1 x tea towel, minimum dimensions 20 x 30in (50 x 76cm), or fabric of your choice cut to those measurements
- [ ] 2 x measuring tapes
- [ ] Scissors
- [ ] Iron
- [ ] 20 x 15in (50 x 38cm) piece of cotton wadding
- [ ] White thread
- [ ] Threads to match your measuring tapes and the stripe in your tea towel

- [ ] Sewing machine
- [ ] Sewing needle and pins
- [ ] Magnetic strip ¼in (5mm) wide, or small magnetic discs ¼in (5mm) in diameter (optional)

Stripe placement (see p.102)

Linen Union GLASS CLOTH Linen Union

FOLD

Linen Union GLASS CLOTH Linen Union

TIP

FEED A LONG STRIP OF ¼IN (5MM) MAGNETIC TAPE (OR THE MAGNETIC DISCS) INTO THE CHANNEL BENEATH THE MEASURING TAPE SO YOU CAN CORRAL YOUR PINS WHILE YOU WORK.

Step 1

Unpick all the hems around your tea towel and press it flat with a hot iron. With the wrong side up and a short end nearest you, fold the top edge of your tea towel down to line up with the bottom edge and press with a hot iron to create a sharp crease. Open out and place your cotton wadding on the bottom half, centred across the width and butting up to the fold crease. Trim it to be ⅜in (1cm) narrower on both sides and along the raw edge at the bottom. Pin or tack and sew down ⅛in (3mm) in from all edges by machine. Remove the pins or tacking and finish off your thread ends.

Step 2

Turn the tea towel over so that the right side is facing you. Fold the top edge down to meet the bottom edge, align all edges and pin or tack. Stitch a ⅜in (1cm) hem around the three open sides, leaving a 6in (15cm) turning gap along the bottom seam – reverse stitch at either side of the turning gap to strengthen it. Remove the pins or tacking and snip the bottom two corners at 90° and the top two at 45°, close to the stitching. Turn out through the turning gap.

Step 3

Tease the corners until they are fairly sharp, then press with a hot iron.

Step 4

Fold in the raw edges of the turning gap by ⅜in (1cm), press with an iron and pin together. Close by hand with small overstitches and white thread and remove the pins.

Step 5

Lay one measuring tape ¼in (5mm) from the bottom and ¾in (2cm) from the left-hand edges. Cut the other end ¾in (2cm) from the right-hand edge. Stitch it in place ⅛in (3mm) from the top and bottom edges of the tape all the way around (stopping short of the metal end if the tape has one) with colour thread on the top of the machine and white thread in the bobbin. Repeat with the other measuring tape along the opposite long edge.

Step 6

Thread the top of the sewing machine with coloured thread to match the stripe on your tea towel. With white thread still in the bobbin, stitch vertical lines in small zigzag stitch 1⅜in (3.5cm) apart between the two measuring tapes. Test out your stitch length on a scrap of fabric until the zigzag measures ⅛in (3mm) wide.

See also:
Topstitching *page 105*
Zigzag stitching *page 105*

I got fed up with the clumsy plastic cover that came with my sewing machine and shoved it to the back of a cupboard many years ago. This alternative cover is a quick make that will keep your machine dust-free between projects. It also has a useful pocket to store sewing basics.

SEWING-MACHINE COVER

Supplies:

(to fit a sewing machine 16 x 11 x 7in/40 x 28 x 18cm)

- [ ] 1 x tea towel, minimum dimensions 20 x 30in (50 x 76cm), or fabric of your choice cut to those measurements
- [ ] 60in (1.5m) of 1in (2.5cm) wide white herringbone tape
- [ ] 1 x A4 sheet of T-shirt transfer paper
- [ ] Scans of the images provided on page 122, or your own digital photographs, of, for example, buttons, thimbles and threads
- [ ] Iron
- [ ] Sewing needle and pins

- [ ] Ruler and pencil or air-erasable pen
- [ ] White thread and thread to match the colour stripe in your tea towel
- [ ] Sewing machine
- [ ] Scissors

Stripe placement (see p.102)

GLASS CLOTH
FOLD   FOLD
GLASS CLOTH

Step 1

Lay your tea towel out in front of you right side up and with one short end nearest you. Cut the two long sides off equally so that you are left with a width of 19in (48.5cm), or the width of your sewing machine plus 3in (7.5cm), and a hemmed length of 30in (76cm), or the measurement from the bottom of the front of your machine, over the top and down to the bottom of the back plus 6in (15cm). Cut any excess from the top edge. Fold this edge down by ⅜in (1cm) twice to form a hem and pin or tack. Sew by machine and press. Turn your fabric over – now wrong side up. Fold the bottom edge up 5½in (14cm). Press the fold with an iron to form the pocket.

Step 2

Pin the pocket in position. Use a ruler and pencil or air-erasable pen to draw a line ⅜in (1cm) in from the right- and left-hand edges from the bottom fold to the top of the pocket. At a point ¾in (2cm) from the bottom corner, cut at an angle of 45° up to the pencil line. Now cut vertically along the line to the top of the pocket through one layer of linen – this will reduce the bulk of fabric layers in the side seam.

Step 3

Sew a ⅜in (1cm) vertical line of zigzag stitch in white in the top centre of the pocket to prevent it sagging.

Step 4

To make the ties, cut your herringbone tape into four equal lengths. Turn one end of each over ⅜in (1cm) and then ⅜in (1cm) again and sew down with a small zigzag stitch in coloured thread to prevent it from fraying.

Step 5

Fold the two long, raw edges in ⅜in (1cm) and then ¾in (2cm) and press with an iron. As you pin or tack them before stitching, insert the raw ends of the four tapes thus: 4½in (11cm) up from each of the four corners, tucked into the side seam fold.

Step 6

Stitch the two side hems by machine using coloured thread and reverse stitching or small zigzag stitching as you pass over the ties to give them extra strength. Remove the pins or tacking.

Step 7

Print the images provided on page 122 (or use your own) onto your T-shirt transfer paper. Remember that the images will be reversed in the transfer process. Cut them out, leaving a ⅛in (3mm) border around each image. Position the images carefully on your pocket front and transfer them using an iron and following the instructions. Peel off the backing paper to reveal the transfers.

See also:
Topstitching *page 105*
Zigzag stitch *page 105*
Iron-on transfers *page 121*

 TIP

I HAVE FOUND IT IS BETTER TO LET THE TRANSFER COOL FULLY BEFORE PEELING OFF THE BACKING PAPER.

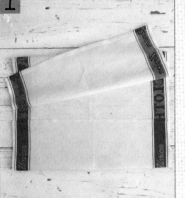

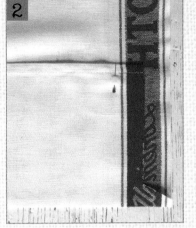

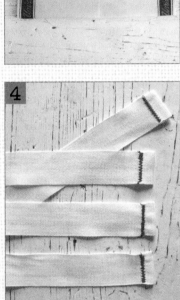

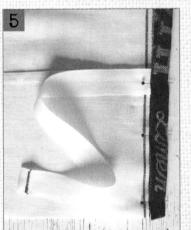

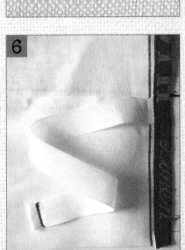

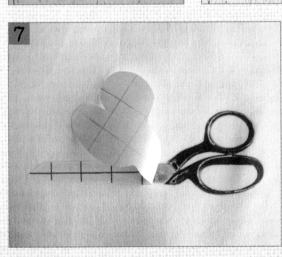

TIP

DON'T BE TEMPTED TO IRON YOUR
TRANSFERS DIRECTLY ONCE THE
PROTECTIVE PAPER IS REMOVED;
FOLLOW THE MANUFACTURER'S
INSTRUCTIONS AT ALL TIMES.

This holder is a neat solution to the tangled ball of string at the back of a drawer – you will always have string to hand hanging by your worktable. Before long, you'll find yourself wrapping and tying things with string where you would previously have used tape or elastic bands.

STRING HOLDER

Supplies:

- ☐ 1 x tea towel, minimum dimensions 30 x 15in (76 x 38cm), or fabric of your choice cut to those measurements
- ☐ 6in (15cm) of 1½in (4cm) wide white herringbone tape
- ☐ 22in (56cm) of 1in (2.5cm) wide white herringbone tape
- ☐ 24in (61cm) of piping cord
- ☐ White thread and thread to match the stripe in your tea towel
- ☐ Sewing and embroidery needles
- ☐ Cotton embroidery threads in various shades to match the stripe in your tea towel

- ☐ Pins and safety pin
- ☐ Sewing machine
- ☐ Iron
- ☐ Scissors
- ☐ String
- ☐ Lightbox

Stripe placement (see p.102)

Step 1

Cut a piece from your tea towel to measure 16 x 10½in (40 x 27cm) – use one hem of the tea towel as your top edge. Fold the fabric in half so it measures 8 x 10½in (20 x 27cm). Press with a hot iron to make a crease and open the fabric out again. Tape a photocopy of the template (found on page 124) in position at the back of your fabric. Trace it up against a windowpane with a fine pencil, or use a lightbox. Position it centred on the left-hand half, using the crease as a guide, and 3in (7.5cm) from the bottom edge. Embroider the motif using chain, couching and blanket stitches. Cut a hole for the string to be threaded through and stitch around its circumference using large blanket stitch.

Step 2

With wrong sides together, fold the piece in half so that the embroidered motif is centrally positioned on the front. Pin or tack and stitch a ⅜in (1cm) hem along the bottom and side seams. Remove the pins or tacking before trimming these two edges down to ¼in (5mm), and the two corners at 45°, and turn inside out. Press the seams flat and stitch ⅜in (1cm) from the edge to make a French seam on the bottom and side.

Step 3

Turn right side out and press with a hot iron. Make a hanging loop by taking 6in (15cm) of the herringbone tape and folding it in half, so it is 6 x ¾in (15 x 2cm). Topstitch down both long sides by machine ⅛in (3mm) in from the edges.

Step 4

Cut a 14¼in (36cm) length of the 1in (2.5cm) herringbone tape. Turn both ends over by ⅜in (1cm). Pin or tack and zigzag back and forth by machine to secure the raw edges. Starting at the centre front of your bag, pin the tape all the way around, aligning the top with the bottom of the wide colour stripe – the two zigzag hemmed ends should meet within ¼in (5mm) of each other at the centre front.

Step 5

Fold the hanging loop in half and tuck behind the tape so that its raw ends are covered and the loop extends over the top edge of the bag. Tack the tape in place before sewing down with a small, close zigzag stitch along the top in colour (to mirror the colour stripe it covers) and in white along the bottom, reverse stitching for strength over the loop ends and at the beginning and end. Remove the pins or tacking.

Step 6

Feed the piping cord through the tape channel with the help of a safety pin. Tie knots at each end or make small drawstring tabs to stop the piping running back into the channel.

See also:

Topstitching *page 105*
French seams *page 107*
Couching stitch *page 116*
Blanket stitch *page 117*
Chain stitch *page 118*

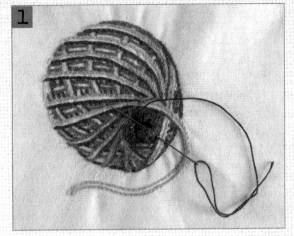

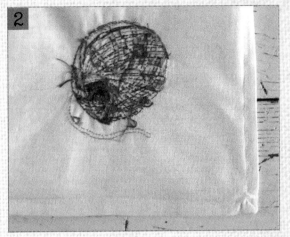

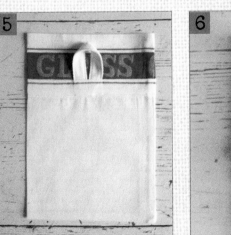

TIP

YOU MAY FIND IT HELPS
TO SLIDE OFF THE ARM
(EXTENSION TABLE) OF
YOUR SEWING MACHINE
SO THAT YOU CAN EASILY
SLIP THE NARROW TOP
OF THE BAG UNDER THE
MACHINE FOOT.

Store and sort your knitting needles in a simple, traditional storage roll. This is based on my grandmother's roll, which perished from constant use many years ago. You could make one on a smaller scale to store crochet hooks. Adjust the depth of the pocket to accommodate your longest needles.

KNITTING-NEEDLE ROLL

Supplies:

- ☐ 1 x tea towel, minimum dimensions 20 x 30in (50 x 76cm), or fabric of your choice cut to those measurements
- ☐ White thread and thread to match the stripe in your tea towel
- ☐ Contrasting colour sewing threads
- ☐ 34½in (88cm) of 1in (2.5cm) wide white herringbone tape
- ☐ Sewing machine
- ☐ Sewing needle and pins
- ☐ Lightbox (optional)
- ☐ Pencil or air-erasable pen
- ☐ Ruler
- ☐ Measuring tape
- ☐ Scissors

Stripe placement (see p.102)

Step 1

Hold your tea towel up against a window or use a lightbox to trace the template from page 124 along one short edge of your tea towel, finishing ¾in (2cm) from one of the shorter hemmed edges. Embroider the numbers using contrasting colour sewing threads for the metric and imperial needle sizes in very small chain stitches. Use French knots for the 'dots'.

Step 2

Retain the two short hems. Cut off the hems on the two long sides of your tea towel; your fabric should now measure 19 x 30in (48.5 x 76cm). Press with a hot iron. With your fabric right side up and the embroidered end nearest you, fold the bottom edge up 10in (25cm). Press and pin or tack the two side seams.

Step 3

Stitch ¾in (2cm) seams along both sides. Remove the pins or tacking and trim one layer of each side seam fabric down to half its depth, ⅜in (1cm), to reduce the bulk in the seam.

Step 4

Fold the wider selvedge over the shorter one. Continue this fold up to the top edge of the fabric. Press and tack. Turn the fabric right side out and press the side seams. Now, following the seam line, continue the fold up to the top edge to create a hem. Pin or tack, and then stitch it all the way from the top to the bottom. As you stitch over the point at the top of the pocket on both sides, change your machine stitch to a small, tight zigzag for ⅜in (1cm); reverse back and forth a few times to add extra strength before removing any pins or tacking.

Step 5

Draw fine lines from the folded bottom edge to the top of the pocket, roughly 1¾in (4.5cm) apart and centred between the embroidered numbers to make the long knitting-needle pockets. With the machine threaded with the contrasting colour thread and the bobbin charged with white thread, stitch the lines starting from the folded edge in straight stitch. When you reach a point level with the bottom of the embroidered numbers, change to a close zigzag stitch, the same width as the fine stripe woven into the sides of the tea towel. Keep the machine foot down but the needle up as you change the stitch function. When you reach the top edge of the pocket, reverse back to the starting point of the zigzag stitching to give the top of the pocket extra strength. Finish off the thread ends by hand with a sewing needle.

Step 6

Fold both ends of the herringbone tape over ¼in (5mm), and ¼in (5mm) again. Pin or tack and stitch by machine back and forth a couple of times to prevent fraying. With the embroidered side of the tea towel face down, lay the tape down horizontally across the tea towel and pin its centre 7in (18cm) from the bottom on the right-hand edge. Pin or tack and stitch down by machine, sewing a rectangle 1⅛ x ¾in (3 x 2cm), then remove any pins. Once your needles are tucked away in their pockets, fold the top edge over 5in (13cm) to keep them in place before rolling it up and tying a bow with the tape.

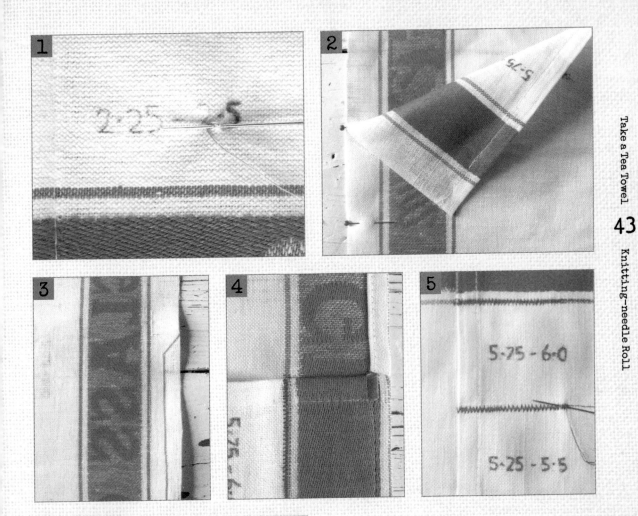

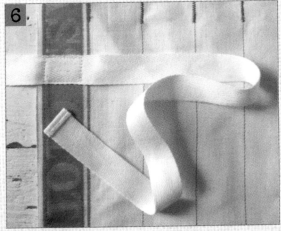

See also:
Straight stitch *page 105*
Zigzag stitch *page 105*
Chain stitch *page 118*
French knots *page 119*

THE LAUNDRY ROOM

Jolly up laundry day with some fresh, bold laundry bags. Hang them on the back of your bedroom or bathroom door. The strong graphic symbols are painted on with fabric paint. Play around using different colours and symbols, making separate bags for coloured, white and delicate washes.

LINEN BAGS

Supplies:

(for each bag)

- [ ] 2 x tea towels, minimum dimensions 20 x 30in (50 x 76cm), or fabric of your choice cut to those measurements
- [ ] Fabric paint
- [ ] Square-ended paintbrush
- [ ] Fine pencil
- [ ] Masking tape
- [ ] Lightbox (optional)
- [ ] Iron
- [ ] White thread
- [ ] Sewing machine
- [ ] Scissors
- [ ] Sewing needle and pins
- [ ] 50in (1.3m) of 1½in (4cm) wide white herringbone tape
- [ ] 100in (2.6m) of piping cord
- [ ] Safety pin

Step 1

Unpick all the hems around your two tea towels and press flat with an iron. Tape a photocopy of the templates of laundry symbols and temperatures (see page 123) in position at the back of your fabric and then trace them with a fine pencil up against a windowpane, or use a lightbox. Place the motifs so that they sit 8in (20cm) from the right-hand edge and 5½in (14cm) from the bottom edge. Using a square-headed paintbrush, carefully fill in the motifs with fabric paint. Turn the fabric as you work so that the lines you are working up to are furthest from you. Take your time and add small amounts of water as you work to keep the paint fluid, as it will thicken as time passes. Follow the manufacturer's instructions for fixing and finishing your fabric paint.

Step 2

Once dry, place your two pieces of linen right sides together, pin or tack and stitch a ¾in (2cm) seam down both long side edges, leaving a 1½in (4cm) gap 3in (8cm) from the top edge on both sides. Remove the pins or tacking and press the seams open and then tuck the raw edges on both sides under by ⅜in (1cm). Stitch all the way along both folded edges by machine. Fold the top edge in by ⅜in (1cm) then ⅜in (1cm) again and stitch close to the edge to make a hem.

Step 3

Turn right side out. Pin or tack the two raw bottom edges together. Stitch a ⅜in (1cm) seam along the bottom edge. Remove pins or tacking, trim to ¼in (5mm) and turn wrong side out. Press with an iron and stitch a ⅜in (1cm) hem to make a French seam.

Step 4

Take 10in (25cm) of the herringbone tape and fold it in half lengthways so that it measures 10 x ¾in (25 x 2cm). Press and machine down each edge to make a hanging loop.

Step 5

Cut the remaining tape to the circumference of the top of your bag plus ¾in (2cm). Overlap the two ends of the herringbone tape by ¾in (2cm) ensuring it is not twisted. Stitch back and forth a few times on the overlap using a zigzag stitch. With the bag wrong side out, pin or tack the herringbone tape around the top, 2¼in (6cm) from the hemmed edge. At the same time, fold the hanging loop in half and insert it under the herringbone tape at the centre of the back of the linen bag (the side without the painted motifs). Sew the tape in place ¼in (5mm) from the top and bottom edges, reverse stitching over the ends of the hanging loop for extra strength. Remove any pins or tacking.

Step 6

Use a safety pin to feed one 50in (1.3m) length of piping cord through the gap in one side seam, all the way around the tape channel and back out through the same gap. Do the same with the remaining length of piping cord, starting and emerging from the gap in the opposite side seam.

Step 7

Knot the ends of the piping cord or make drawstring tabs.

1

See also:
Zigzag stitch *page 105*
French seams *page 107*
Making drawstring tabs *page 114*
Fabric painting *page 120*

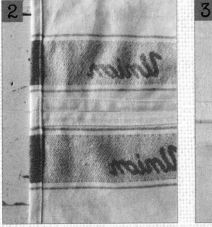

2

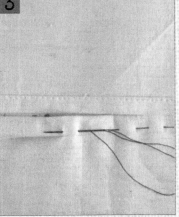

3

4

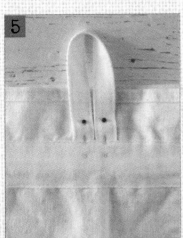

5

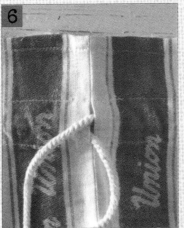

6

7

Keep sets of linen for your beds in individual bags to simplify that rummage in the linen cupboard and avoid that frustrating refolding of the wrong size sheet or duvet cover. It really does save time since you generally launder sets of linen together – simply fold them away in sets.

BEDLINEN ENVELOPES

Supplies:

(for each envelope)

- ☐ 1 x tea towel, minimum dimensions 20 x 30in (50 x 76cm), or fabric of your choice cut to size
- ☐ Pencil or air-erasable pen
- ☐ Lightbox (optional)
- ☐ 3 x ¾in (2cm) diameter linen or Dorset buttons
- ☐ 43in (110cm) of 1in (2.5cm) wide white herringbone tape
- ☐ White thread
- ☐ Sewing and embroidery needles, and pins
- ☐ Scissors

- ☐ Embroidery cotton to match the colour stripe in your tea towel
- ☐ Sewing machine
- ☐ Buttonhole foot (optional)
- ☐ Iron

Stripe placement (see p.102)

Step 1

Unpick the short hems of your tea towel and press flat. Lay it out vertically and tape a photocopy of the hearts (see template on page 124) in position at the back of your fabric, centred on both the width and length. Trace the templates with a fine pencil up against a windowpane, or use a lightbox. Stitch the outline of the hearts with embroidery cotton in chain stitch. Then fill in the stitched outlines with French knots. Use one (single), two (double) or three (king size) hearts to indicate your bedlinen set sizes.

Step 2

With the wrong side up, fold the bottom raw edge up ⅜in (1cm). Cut a piece of herringbone tape ¾in (2cm) longer than the width of your linen and pin or tack along the bottom edge to align with the folded edge and cover the raw edge. Turn each end of the tape under by ⅜in (1cm).

Step 3

Stitch ⅛in (3mm) in all the way around the tape by machine and remove any pins or tacking.

Step 4

Repeat Step 2 with the raw top edge of your tea towel. Either by hand or by machine, stitch three buttonholes along the bottom edge (at right angles to the hemmed edge) to fit your buttons: one centrally, and the other two 3in (7.5cm) to either side.

Step 5

With the right side of your tea towel facing you, fold the top (buttonhole) edge down 4¾in (12cm), then fold the bottom edge up roughly 9½in (24cm)

so that the two strips of tape overlap each other by about 1in (2.5cm) – the width of the herringbone tape. Press with a hot iron.

Step 6

Pin or tack the side seams of the tea towel. Sew a ⅜in (1cm) seam along the left- and right-hand sides, reverse stitching at the beginning and end and over the ends of the tape where the fabric is several layers thick to give it extra strength. Remove any pins or tacking.

Step 7

Now make your four box corners. With your work still right side out, flatten each of the four corners, pressing the side seams open. When flattening each corner, align the seams with the ironed crease marks from step 5 to make sure they are symmetrical, and pin carefully.

Step 8

On each corner, draw a line 1½in (4cm) in from the point of the corner. Stitch across each line, reversing at both ends, and trim the corner off ⅛in (5mm) from the stitching. Remove the pins.

Step 9

Turn the fabric wrong side out and press the box corner seams. Sew ⅜in (1cm) seams along each box corner seam to enclose the raw edges and create French seams.

Step 10

Turn right side out and stitch the three buttons in position to correspond with the buttonholes.

1

2

3

4

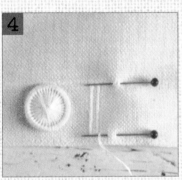

5

6

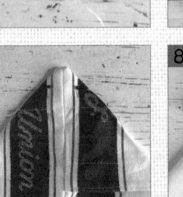

7

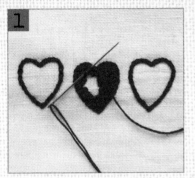

8

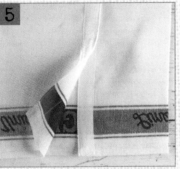

9

10

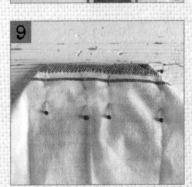

See also:

Dorset buttons *page 66*

French seams *page 107*

Making box corners *page 108*

Buttonholes *page 113*

Chain stitch *page 118*

French knots *page 119*

There's nothing better than sunshine and a breeze to keep laundry fresh, white and crisp. This clothes-peg bag is a pretty, ageless favourite, both simple and practical. On laundry days, keep it hanging on your washing line so your pegs are close to hand.

CLOTHES-PEG BAG

Supplies:

- [ ] 1 x tea towel, minimum dimensions 20 x 26in (50 x 66cm), or fabric of your choice cut to those measurements
- [ ] 1 x wooden coat hanger
- [ ] Small saw (junior hacksaw)
- [ ] Fine glass paper
- [ ] Ruler and pencil or air-erasable pen
- [ ] A4 paper
- [ ] White thread and thread to match the stripe in your tea towel

- [ ] Lightbox (optional)
- [ ] Thread in a contrasting colour
- [ ] Sewing needles and pins
- [ ] Sewing machine
- [ ] Scissors
- [ ] Iron

Stripe placement (see p.102)

Step 1

Cut equal amounts off both 'arms' of your coat hanger so that it measures 9¾in (25cm) across. Use a small piece of glass paper to take any sharpness off the edges.

Step 2

Unpick the hems of your tea towel and press. Lay it out horizontally in front of you, right side down, and fold the left-hand edge across by 11in (28cm). Place the coat hanger on the fabric 9¾in (25cm) above the bottom edge and ¾in (2cm) in from the left-hand edge. Draw along its top curve with a fine pencil or air-erasable pen, marking the position of the wire hook. Now draw a vertical line up to and ¾in (2cm) to the right of the right-hand edge of the coat hanger. Cut out these pieces of linen – 11 x 16in (28 x 40cm).

Step 3

Cut one piece shorter by re-drawing the top curve 1½in (4cm) lower down and cutting along it. This will be the back of your peg bag. Cut horizontally across your second piece 5½in (14cm) below the top edge – you now have two pieces for the front of your bag. Hold your tea towel up against a window

or use a lightbox to trace the pegs template (see page 125) onto the larger front piece, sitting 5in (13cm) from the bottom edge. Embroider the motifs in colour thread with tiny chain and backstitches.

Step 4

Place the larger front piece down right side up and with the bottom edge nearest you. Place the smaller piece on top, aligning the raw top edges, and pin or tack in position. Sew a ¾in (2cm) seam 2¼in (6cm) in from either edge – thus leaving a 6½in (16cm) gap in the middle. Reverse stitch at both ends of each short seam for extra strength and remove any pins or tacking. With the wrong side facing you, press the seam open. Tuck the raw edges under ⅜in (1cm) along the seams and the central gap. Stitch down by machine.

Step 5

Now machine a horizontal line of small, close zigzag stitches in colour the width of the opening gap and ¼in (5mm) below it.

Step 6

Lay the front and back pieces right sides together, pin or tack and sew a ⅜in (1cm) seam all the way around, leaving a ¾in (2cm) gap at the centre of the top curve where you marked the position of the metal hook. Remove any pins or tacking. Zigzag around all the seams (apart from the hook hole at the top, of course) to reduce fraying.

Step 7

Turn right side out and reinforce the hole for the hook with topstitching.

See also:
Topstitching *page 105*
Zigzag stitch *page 105*
French seams *page 107*
Backstitch *page 117*
Chain stitch *page 118*

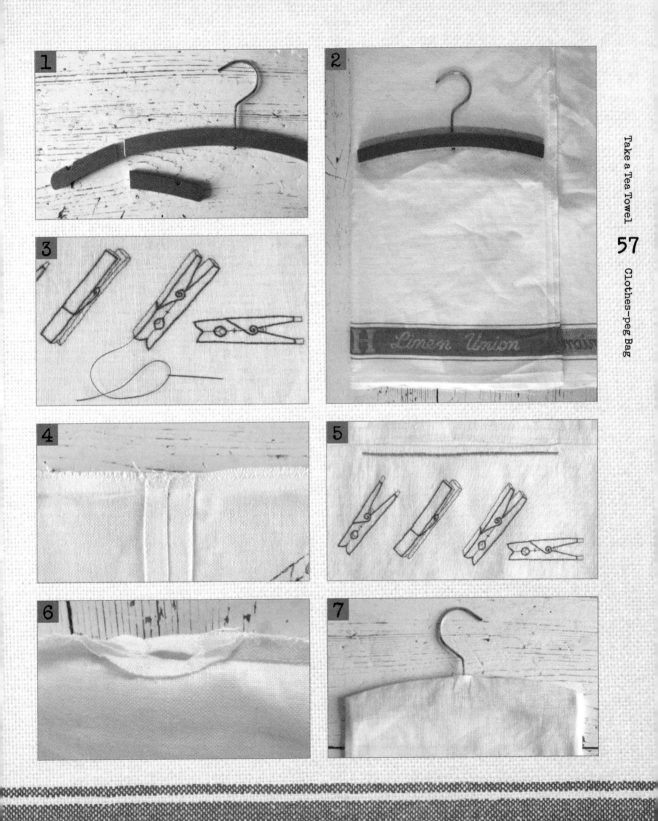

Keep clothes fresh and dust-free. These items are particularly useful for clothing that stays tucked away in a wardrobe for months, waiting for the right weather or occasion. Sweet little hanging hearts filled with dried lavender or spices keep things smelling fresh and help repel moths.

COAT-HANGER COVER

Supplies:

- [ ] 1 x tea towel, minimum dimensions 20 x 30in (50 x 76cm), or fabric of your choice cut to those measurements
- [ ] 40in (101.5cm) of rickrack to match the colour of your tea towel stripe
- [ ] 7in (18cm) of 1in (2.5cm) wide herringbone tape
- [ ] 2 x ³⁄₈in (1cm) diameter buttons
- [ ] White thread
- [ ] Sewing needle and pins
- [ ] Sewing machine
- [ ] Scissors

- [ ] Crochet hook
- [ ] Pencil
- [ ] Iron
- [ ] Dried lavender (or spices of your choice)
- [ ] Wooden coat hanger

Stripe placement (see p.102)

GLASS CLOTH

FOLD

GLASS CLOTH

COAT-HANGER COVER
Step 1

Unpick the long edges of your tea towel. Fold your fabric in half, wrong sides together, so that the two raw edges are aligned, and press. Lay the fabric down with the raw edges nearest you and the fold furthest away. Place your coat hanger 4in (10cm) above the raw edges. Use a pencil to draw around the shape of the hanger. Mark another line 1½in (4cm) outside this line for your seam allowance. Join the ends of your curved lines to the bottom edge with vertical lines. Cut out your fabric. Cut two lengths of rickrack the width of your fabric pieces.

Step 2

With right sides facing, take one piece of fabric and tack a piece of rickrack 2in (5cm) above the bottom raw edge. Fold the bottom edge up ¼in (5mm), then again ½in (1.25cm). Adjust the measurements if necessary so that your folded hem covers half of the rickrack's width.

Step 3

Pin or tack the hem down and press with a hot iron. Topstitch your hem ⅛in (3mm) in from the folded edge. Remove any pins or tacking. Repeat with the other piece of fabric. With wrong sides facing, fold the top edges over by ¼in (5mm), then ¼in (5mm) again. Press, pin or tack and stitch by machine to hem. Remove any pins or tacking.

Step 4

Place both sides together, wrong sides facing. Pin or tack and sew a ⅜in (1cm) seam along both sides, taking care to align the top and bottom hemmed edges. Remove any pins or tacking and trim both side seams to ¼in (5mm).

Step 5

Turn inside out and press both side seams. Pin or tack and sew a ⅜in (1cm) seam along each side, reverse stitching at each end for strength.

Step 6

Remove any pins or tacking and finish off. Turn right side out and press.

LAVENDER HEART
Step A

Cut two heart shapes from your scraps (see template on page 125). Tack rickrack all around the edge of one heart shape, starting and finishing at the centre top with ¾in (2cm) excess at either end.

Step B

Place the second heart on top and pin or tack all the way around. Machine stitch a ¼in (5mm) hem, leaving a 1⅜in (3.5cm) gap at one side and a ⅜in (1cm) gap at the centre top. Remove tacking.

Step C

Turn right side out. Use a crochet hook to push and tease the seams before pressing it with a hot iron. Insert the hook in through the side turning gap and out again through the hole in the centre top. Pull the rickrack ends through to the inside of your heart.

Step D

Fold the raw edges in at the turning gap, then stuff with dried lavender. Close with small hand stitches, taking care to stitch through the rickrack and to catch both sides of the fabric. Fold the tape in half and stitch ⅛in (3mm) in from the edges to make your hanging loop. Fold the ends under and stitch by hand to either side of the heart ⅜in (1cm) from the centre top, anchoring it with a button on either side.

TIP

IT IS BETTER TO MAKE YOUR COAT-HANGER COVER TOO LOOSE THAN TOO TIGHT.

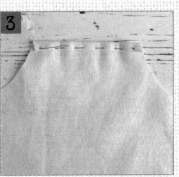

See also:
French seams *page 107*
Sewing on buttons *page 112*

THE BATHROOM

This simple panel for a window or door gives a crisp, clean and uncluttered look to a small room. Make your own pretty cotton Dorset buttons to decorate the top edge and secure the hanging loops. Several tea towels can be stitched together to make larger panels.

WINDOW PANEL

Supplies:

(finished size: 20 x 28¼in/50 x 72cm)

☐ 1 x tea towel, minimum dimensions 20 x 30in (50 x 76cm), or fabric of your choice cut to those measurements

☐ 31½in (80cm) of 1in (2.5cm) wide white herringbone tape

☐ Fine white knitting or crochet cotton

☐ Embroidery needle

☐ 5 x ¾in (2cm) diameter curtain rings

☐ White thread

☐ Sewing needle and pins

☐ Sewing machine

☐ Scissors

☐ Iron

DORSET BUTTONS

Step A

The instructions for these sweet little buttons are exactly the same as those first used in the 17th century. Make five buttons using the cotton yarn and small curtain rings. Thread an embroidery needle with your thread. Tie one end of your thread onto the curtain ring. Work in blanket stitch around the circumference of the ring, covering the raw knot end with your first few stitches.

Step B

Make sure you make enough stitches to completely cover the ring. Stitch into your first stitch again to hide the join. Slide the stitches around the ring so that the outside blanket stitch ridge is now on the inside of the ring and the outside edge is completely smooth.

Step C

Wrap your thread around the ring from top to bottom. Turn the ring slightly and wrap the thread around again. Continue until you have wrapped ten times to create the spokes of the wheel. At this point the threads will look somewhat random; use the end of your needle to tweak and reposition them so they are dispersed evenly around the ring. Make a couple of stitches in the centre of the wheel to secure the spokes and even them out.

Step D

Using backstitch, work your way around the spokes in a clockwise spiral from the centre outwards. Thread ends can be finished off, but leave one or two of them long to fix your button to the fabric.

WINDOW PANEL

Step 1

Make five hanging loops: fold your herringbone tape in half across its width to make a strip 31½in (80cm) x ½in (1.25cm). Press with a hot iron and topstitch down the open side ⅛in (3mm) in from the edge to close. Cut into five lengths of 6½in (16cm). Retain the long side seams of your tea towel. Unpick the two short seams of your tea towel and press flat. With your fabric wrong side up and a short end nearest you, fold the bottom edge up ⅜in (1cm), and then 1⅜in (3.5cm) and press with a hot iron. Pin or tack and stitch by machine to hem, reverse stitching at either end. Remove any pins or tacking.

Step 2

Turn the fabric so that the other short (top) end is nearest you. Fold the raw edge under ⅜in (1cm), then 1⅜in (3.5cm) again and press with a hot iron. Fold the five lengths of tape in half and slot their raw ends under your folded hem, two of them ⅜in (1cm) from either side seam and the remaining three equally spaced between them. Tack or pin along the hem.

Step 3

Stitch the hem by machine, reverse stitching at either end. Remove any pins or tacking and press the hanging loops upwards so that they project above the top hem of your panel. Turn your fabric over. Using the 'tail' threads from your Dorset buttons and an embroidery needle, stitch a button in place at the bottom of each loop, stitching through all layers of the hem and the hanging loops, thus securing them in position.

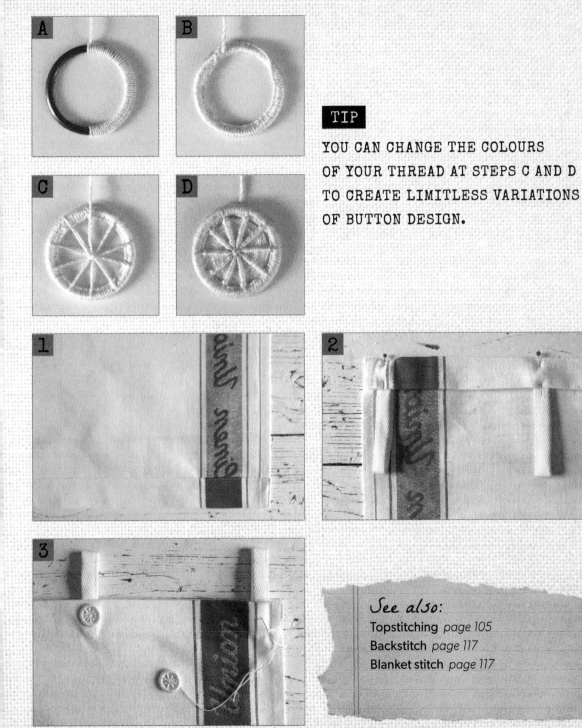

TIP

YOU CAN CHANGE THE COLOURS
OF YOUR THREAD AT STEPS C AND D
TO CREATE LIMITLESS VARIATIONS
OF BUTTON DESIGN.

See also:
Topstitching *page 105*
Backstitch *page 117*
Blanket stitch *page 117*

A striking 'red cross' chair seat for an emergency! A small, simple chair is very useful in a bathroom, and any chair with a drop-in seat like this one from the 1950s is perfect for freshening up with a bold linen cover. Play around with the design by using different colour tea towels.

CHAIR SEAT

Supplies:

- [ ] 2 x tea towels, minimum dimensions 20 x 20in (50 x 50cm each), or fabric of your choice cut to those measurements
- [ ] 2 x pieces of wadding, 4in (10cm) larger than the dimensions of your chair seat
- [ ] Measuring tape
- [ ] Scissors
- [ ] White thread
- [ ] Sewing needle and pins

- [ ] Sewing machine
- [ ] Herringbone tape
- [ ] Sheet of newspaper and pencil
- [ ] Staple gun and staples

TIP

PROTECT YOUR FINISHED SEAT WITH STAIN RETARDANT SPRAY

Stripe placement (see p.102)

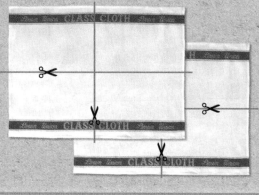

Step 1

Unpick all four hems on your tea towels and press flat. Cut each into quarters across their vertical and horizontal axes. Trim along one side to within ⅜in (1cm) of the colour stripe. Take two pieces that mirror each other and put right sides together so that their stripes match up as accurately as possible. Pin or tack in position. Sew a ⅜in (1cm) seam along the edge of the stripe, then remove any pins or tacking and press the seam open with a hot iron.

Step 2

Repeat step 1 with the remaining three pairs of fabric pieces. Take one of your four pieces of linen and lay it down, right side up and with the stripe positioned vertically. Take the left- and right-hand corners nearest you and fold them in at 45° so that their raw edges meet at the central seam. Press with a hot iron. Open out again.

Step 3

Repeat step 2 with the remaining three pieces of linen. Take two pieces of linen and lay them on top of each other, right sides together, ensuring that the lettering is the same way round for both pieces and that their ironed creases are aligned.

Step 4

Pin or tack and then stitch a seam ⅜in (1cm) inside the crease at 45° to the stripe. Remove any pins or tacking and trim the seam ⅜in (1cm) from the stitching (that is, along the pressed crease) and press the seam open. Repeat with the remaining two pieces of linen. Cut along the two 45° creases of one piece and place it right sides together with the stripes aligning on top of the other piece.

Step 5

Cut the excess two triangles of fabric off from the bottom piece. Pin or tack the pieces together, then sew a seam ⅜in (1cm) in from the cut edge, remove any pins or tacking and press all seams open.

Step 6

Take the loose seat out of your chair frame. Make a pattern for your seat by drawing around it onto a sheet of newspaper. Add 2in (5cm) all the way around and cut out. Fold into quarters, crease it and open it out flat again. Use the pattern creases to centre it on your prepared fabric, laying the creases along the seams that run horizontally and vertically. Pin the pattern in position and cut out the fabric. Remove the pattern and cut it down by 2in (5cm) to your original outline. Cut one piece of wadding this size. Draw a vertical and a horizontal line on the underneath of your seat base, dividing it into four equal parts. Place your fabric face down on a solid surface with the wadding centred on top of it.

Step 7

Centre your chair seat upside down on top of the linen and wadding. Starting at the centre of the top furthest from you, pull the fabric over the edge of the seat towards the middle of the base, making sure the centre of your fabric stripe aligns with your pencil lines, and secure with a staple. Do the same directly opposite at the centre of the bottom edge nearest you. Turn the seat 90° and repeat with the sides of the seat. Work methodically, stapling from the centre of each side towards the edges and turning the seat as you progress.

Step 8

Keep the tension in the fabric even, avoiding tucks and wrinkles. Drop the seat pad into the chair frame.

This is just the thing for storing toiletries – a practical wash bag that is surprisingly capacious. Ripstop kite fabric used as a lining means that it is waterproof and can easily be wiped clean, and that your suitcase contents are protected from a damp flannel or toothbrush.

WASH BAG

Supplies:

- ☐ 1 x tea towel, minimum dimensions 20 x 26in (50 x 66cm), or fabric of your choice cut to those measurements
- ☐ 14 x 18½in (35 x 47cm) of white ripstop fabric
- ☐ White thread and thread to match the stripe in your tea towel

- ☐ 1 x 13½in (34cm) white zipper
- ☐ Scissors
- ☐ Sewing needle and pins
- ☐ Sewing machine
- ☐ Zipper foot
- ☐ Iron

TIP

YOU COULD USE A PIECE OF
SHOWER CURTAIN INSTEAD
OF THE RIPSTOP KITE FABRIC.

Stripe placement (see p.102)

Step 1

Lay the tea towel right side up and with a long edge nearest you. Cut both sides off with vertical cuts and trim off top and bottom ends, so that the fabric measures 13¾ x 18½in (35 x 47cm). Place the zipper, right side down, along the top edge with its opening on the left, aligning its top edge ¾in (2cm) below the top edge of the linen. Lay one of the short edges of the ripstop fabric over the zipper, with its top edge ⅜in (1cm) below the edge of the linen. Pin or tack and stitch by machine.

Step 2

Turn your fabrics so they are wrong sides facing. Press from the linen side. Now with the linen right side up and the zipper edge nearest you, fold the bottom edge up to align with the top edge (the zipper opening on the right). Tack the unstitched side of the zipper in place along the colour stripe. Turn over and fold up the ripstop lining and pin or tack to align with the top edge of the zipper. Stitch by machine. Remove any pins or tacking.

Step 3

Turn your fabrics right side out. Press from the linen side and topstitch along either side of the zipper.

Step 4

With a small, close zigzag stitch, sew two ¾in (2cm) 'stopper' lines at either end of your zipper, at right angles to the zipper's teeth.

Step 5

Make a 'pull' by cutting a strip of linen 4¾ x 2in (12 x 5cm) from your scraps. With the wrong side up, fold the strip in half (it will now measure 4¾ x 1in/12 x 2.5cm) and press. Open it out and fold the two long edges in to meet the central crease. Fold

the two sides in along the central crease again to form a strip 4¾ x ½in (12 x 1.25cm). Pin or tack and topstitch along both sides ⅛in (3mm) in from the folded edges. Remove any pins or tacking. Flatten your tube of fabric right sides out with the zipper centred horizontally in front of you and with the zipper opening on the left. Pin the folded pull on either side of the left-hand end of the zipper with the raw edges aligning and the loop to the right.

Step 6

Make a 'tab' by cutting a 2¾ x 2¾in (7 x 7cm) scrap of linen from step 1. Fold it in half, right sides together. Machine stitch the longer sides, remove any pins or tacking and turn right side out. Press. Pin the tab over the zipper on the right-hand side with the raw edges aligning and the tab to the left.

Step 7

With the zipper half open for turning out, stitch a ⅜in (1cm) seam along both ends, reverse stitching over the tab and the pull for extra strength. Trim the side seams to ¼in (5mm). Turn your bag inside out and tease the seams flat (do NOT iron). Pin or tack and stitch ⅜in (1cm) seams along either side to create French seams. Remove any pins or tacking.

Step 8

Open right side out and make four box corners. Pin or tack and stitch a seam at 90°, 2½in (6.5cm) in from each corner point.

Step 9

Remove any pins or tacking and trim ¼in (5mm) from the stitch lines and turn the bag inside out. Tease the seams flat (do NOT iron). Pin or tack and stitch ⅜in (1cm) seams along each corner. Remove any pins or tacking and turn right side out.

TIP

MAKE SURE YOU LEAVE
THE ZIPPER AT LEAST
2IN (5CM) OPEN WHEN
SEWING IT IN.

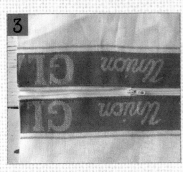

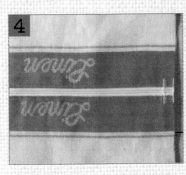

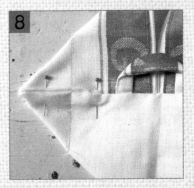

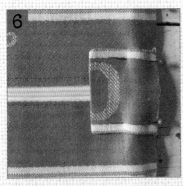

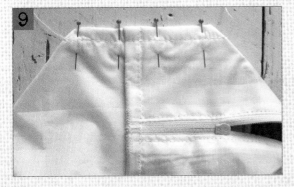

See also:

This practical bathroom bag is perfect when you are away from home. It rolls up for travelling and hangs open once you arrive, and has waterproof pockets for your toothbrush, toothpaste, comb, flannel and soap. Adjust the proportions of the pockets to suit your own needs.

HANGING ROLL

Supplies:

- ☐ 1 x tea towel, minimum dimensions 20 x 28½in (50 x 73cm), or fabric of your choice cut to those measurements
- ☐ 10½ x 28½in (26.5 x 73cm) of white ripstop fabric
- ☐ White thread
- ☐ 1 x 10in (25cm) white zipper
- ☐ 1 x 1in (2.5cm) Dorset button (see page 66 for making instructions)
- ☐ 1 x small button
- ☐ Scissors
- ☐ Sewing needle and pins
- ☐ Sewing machine
- ☐ Zipper foot
- ☐ Iron

Stripe placement (see p.102)

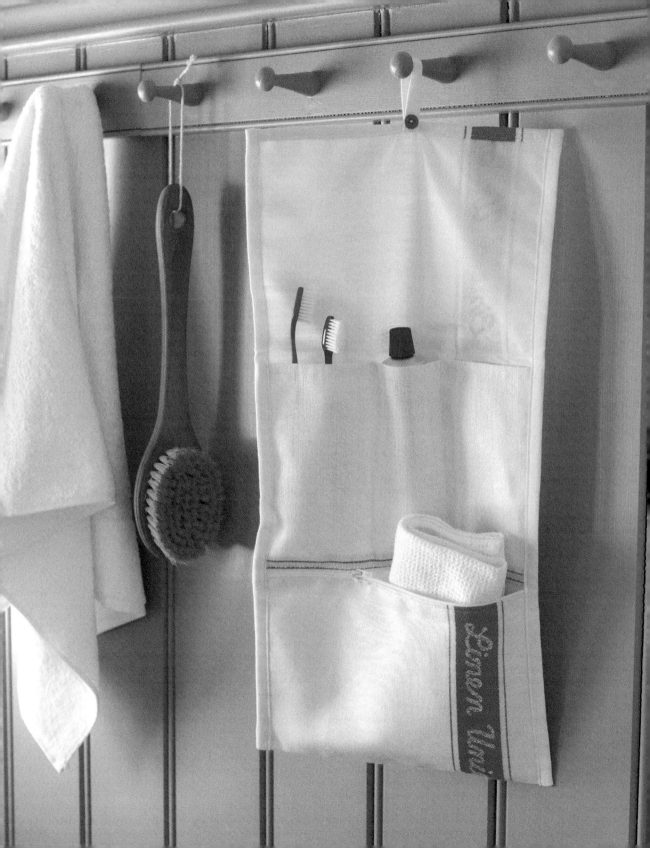

Step 1

Unpick the hems around your tea towel and press flat. Lay it right side down vertically in front of you. Mark a line 12in (30cm) in from the left-hand edge and cut along it. Take this piece and lay it out horizontally. Trim it to measure 10¼ x 8in (26 x 20cm). Sew along the bottom edge with a large zigzag stitch to reduce fraying. With wrong side up, fold up the bottom long edge ⅜in (1cm) and press. Fold the top long edge down ⅜in (1cm), then ⅜in (1cm) again. Press. This is the middle pocket piece.

Step 2

Cut a rectangle of white ripstop fabric 10¼ x 6½in (26 x 16cm) and lay it along the back of the middle pocket piece, tucking the long edges inside the pressed edges of the linen. Pin or tack the edges down over the ripstop and stitch the two hems.

Step 3

Take the main piece of fabric, trim it to measure 12 x 28½in (30 x 73cm) and lay it down vertically, right side up. Open the zipper and tack one side along the top raw edge of fabric. Cut a piece of ripstop 10¼ x 28in (26 x 71cm). Align one short end with the top of your linen and zip. Pin or tack it in position. Use a zipper foot on your machine to stitch along this seam, ⅛in (3mm) from the zipper teeth.

Step 4

Fold the fabric over so the wrong sides are together and, with the linen facing you, press with an iron. Tack through all layers just below the zipper teeth.

Step 5

Topstitch ⅛in (3mm) from the edge of the linen below the zipper, then close it. Turn your work over so that the ripstop is facing you and the zipper edge is nearest to you. Fold the bottom edge up 6½in (16cm). Place the middle pocket piece right side up above the zipper and overlapping to within ⅛in (3mm) of the top set of zipper teeth. Pin or tack, then topstitch, ⅛in (3mm) from the edge.

Step 6

Mark two vertical lines on the top of the middle pocket piece. Stitch them, changing to a small, tight zigzag for the top ⅜in (1cm).

Step 7

Take 5½in (14cm) of tape and fold it in half to measure 5½ x ½in (14 x 1.25cm). Topstitch along both edges to make a loop. With the work laid out vertically, ripstop side up, fold the top edge of the ripstop down and out of the way. Then fold the top edge of the linen down ⅜in (1cm) and then ⅜in (1cm) again and press. Fold the ripstop back up and trim to fit under the fold of the linen, then tuck it underneath. Fold the loop in half and tuck it under the hem in the centre. Pin or tack, then stitch the hem down.

Step 8

Cut two lengths of tape, ¾in (2cm) longer than the sides of your work. Fold the short ends in ⅜in (1cm) and press. Fold in half, now ½in (1.25cm) wide, encase the long raw edge of the linen and ripstop with the tape, tucking them firmly into the crease.

Step 9

Topstitch ⅛in (3mm) in from the edge of the tape through all layers of fabric. Fold the hanging loop up over the top hem and secure with a small button.

Step 10

Stitch your Dorset button centrally and 6¾in (17cm) up from the bottom edge on the back.

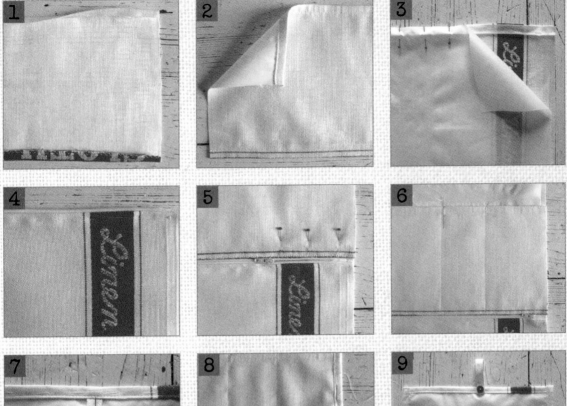

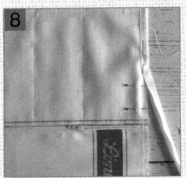

See also:
Dorset buttons *page 66*
Topstitching *page 105*
Inserting a zipper *page 109*
Binding edges *page 110*

THE KITCHEN

A traditional apron with clean lines and a nod to the 1950s.
Pleats at the waist give it a feminine shape, while the addition
of D-rings mean that you can always have a cloth available
for wiping your hands or carrying hot plates to the table.

COOK'S APRON

Supplies:

- [ ] 1 x tea towel, minimum dimensions
      20 x 30in (50 x 76cm), or fabric
      of your choice cut to those
      measurements
- [ ] 72in (2m) of 1½in (4cm) white
      herringbone tape
- [ ] 2 x 1½in (4cm) D-rings
- [ ] White thread
- [ ] Sewing machine
- [ ] Sewing needle and pins
- [ ] Scissors
- [ ] Iron
- [ ] Pencil and ruler

Stripe placement (see p.102)

Step 1

Cut 6in (15cm) from the herringbone tape and feed it through the two D-rings, aligning the raw ends. Set the sewing machine to a close zigzag stitch and machine back and forth a few times ⅜in (1cm) from the folded end to encase the rings. You may have to use a zipper foot for this depending on the width of your standard foot and the diameter of the D-rings.

Step 2

Lay your linen tea towel wrong side up and vertically in front of you. Draw a line 23in (58cm) from the left-hand edge and cut along it. Put the narrower section of fabric aside for making the pocket later. Fold the raw right-hand edge in ⅜in (1cm) and then ⅜in (1cm) again. Press, pin or tack and sew a hem by machine. Remove any pins or tacking.

Step 3

To make the pocket: cut a 7 x 9in (18 x 23cm) piece from the bottom section of fabric that you put aside. Fold the top edge over ⅜in (1cm) then ⅜in (1cm) again. Press, pin or tack and stitch a hem by machine. Remove any pins or tacking. With the wrong side up, fold the three raw edges of the pocket piece in ⅜in (1cm) and press. Make a tab from a scrap of linen 4 x 2½ in (10 x 6.5cm). Pin the pocket in position on the front of the apron, 1¾in (4.5cm) in from the right-hand edge and 4¾in (12cm) from the bottom. Fold the tab in half and tuck it under the right-hand edge of the pocket, 2¾in (7cm) from the pocket top.

Step 4

Topstitch the pocket on by machine, reversing back and forth at the right- and left-hand top corners for extra strength. Remove any pins or tacking. Find the centre of the top edge of your apron. Measure out from this point to either side 5½in (14cm), then mark five more points 1⅛in (3cm) apart. Make three pleats on each side, with their folds facing away from the centre.

Step 5

Pin or tack and machine stitch ⅜in (1cm) from the top edge to hold the pleats. Remove any pins or tacking and press the herringbone tape in half along its length. Align its centre with the centre at the top of your apron. Fold it over the top edge to encase the top of the apron and pin or tack. Work away from the centre to either end of the tape, inserting the D-rings' tape 2¾in (7cm) from the left-hand edge. When you reach the ends of the tape, fold the raw edges in ⅜in (1cm). Stitch by machine down one end of the tape tie, along the bottom edge of the tape, across the apron front through all the layers of fabric, along the tape and up the other end. Remove any pins or tacking and finish off all threads by hand with a sewing needle.

See also:
Topstitching *page 105*
Zigzag stitch *page 105*
Making drawstring tabs *page 114*

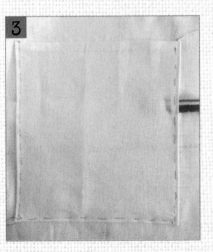

TIP

YOU WILL HAVE
ENOUGH FABRIC TO
MAKE TWO POCKETS OR
A WIDER CENTRAL ONE.

This strong shopping tote fits comfortably over your shoulder and folds up small enough to be tucked into a shopping basket. It has strong herringbone tape handles for long-lasting use, and the practical dip-dyed 'scuff bottom' stops the base looking too grubby.

TOTE BAG

Supplies:

- [ ] 1 x tea towel, minimum dimensions 20 x 30in (50 x 76cm), or fabric of your choice cut to those measurements
- [ ] 96in (2.5m) of 1½in (4cm) wide white herringbone tape
- [ ] Hand dye (see packaging for any other items needed for dying)
- [ ] White thread (100% cotton)
- [ ] Sewing needle and pins
- [ ] Sewing machine
- [ ] Scissors
- [ ] Iron

Stripe placement (see p.102)

GLASS CLOTH

FOLD

GLASS CLOTH

DIP DYEING
Step A

Unpick all the edges of the tea towel and press flat with a hot iron. Before dying, place the bucket that will contain your dye on the floor between two chairs. Fill it with the same amount of water required to make up your dye later. Lay a broom handle across the two chairs and measure the distance between it and the surface of the water – this is to ascertain the height of the dip-dyed area of your finished fabric. At this point, calculate whether you need to raise the dye container, using a pile of large books or magazines. Pre-wash your tea towel (without using fabric softener) to remove any finish that could affect the dye. Prepare the dye following the instructions on the packaging. Wrap the top raw edge of the damp fabric around the broom handle and pin it in place. Give the dye one last stir and lower the bottom of the fabric gently into the dye, resting the broom handle across the two chairs.

Step B

During the hour it takes the dye to take, either lower or raise the towel in the dye to grade the colour strength. When the dyeing time is up, remove the towel, rinse and wash it following the dye instructions. Once given its final wash, hang your fabric out to dry and then press with a hot iron.

See also:
Topstitching *page 105*
French seams *page 107*

ASSEMBLING THE TOTE
Step 1

With wrong sides together, fold the tea towel in half so that it now measures 20 x 15in (50 x 38cm). Pin or tack and stitch a ⅜in (1cm) hem along the bottom and side seams. Remove any pins or tacking. Trim these two edges down to ¼in (5mm), and the two corners at 45°, and turn inside out. Press the seams flat and stitch ⅜in (1cm) from the edge to make a French seam along the bottom and one side.

Step 2

With the bag still inside out, fold the top raw edge over 1in (2.5cm) and press. Cut a length of herringbone tape the circumference of the top of your bag plus 2in (5cm). Pin it around the top just below the fold and covering the raw edge of the linen. Fold the end of the tape under and cover the raw beginning of the tape with this folded end.

Step 3

Cut two 32in (82cm) lengths of tape for the handles. Position the handles 4¾in (12cm) in from each side and tuck them up under the pinned tape and into the pressed hem so that their raw ends butt up to the top fold of the bag. Pin or tack the handles in position, making sure they are not twisted.

Step 4

Stitch along the hem by machine, reversing over the four handle ends for extra strength. Remove any pins or tacking. Fold the handles up and pin or tack in place. Stitch around the bag, ⅛in (3mm) below the top and bottom edges of the tape. Fold the handles upwards. Reinforce the handles by reverse stitching back and forth in line with the two lines of stitching on the herringbone tape below. Remove the pins and turn right side out and press.

TIP

TO ACHIEVE AN 'OMBRÉ' EFFECT, REPEAT STEPS 1 AND 2, CREATING RANDOM DESIGNS AND OVER-DYEING WITH DIFFERENT COLOURS.

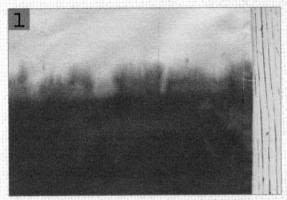

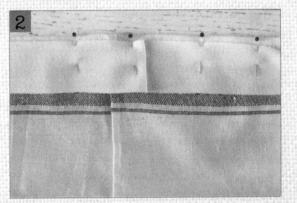

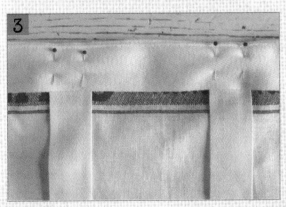

Three small bags are made from just one tea towel. Pretty little sacks to store larder staples such as fresh garlic, ginger and herbs. You can keep them in the fridge, but they are pretty enough for display too. Use different coloured tapes for the handles to differentiate their contents.

VEGETABLE BAGS

Supplies:

(to make three bags)

- ☐ 1 x tea towel, minimum dimensions 20 x 30in (50 x 76cm), or fabric of your choice cut to those measurements

- ☐ 60in (1.5m) of ¾in (2cm) wide white herringbone tape

- ☐ 60in (1.5m) of ¾in (2cm) wide herringbone tape to match the stripe in your tea towel

- ☐ White thread and thread to match the stripe in your tea towel

- ☐ Pencil or air-erasable pen
- ☐ Sewing needle and pins
- ☐ Sewing machine
- ☐ Scissors
- ☐ Iron

Stripe placement (see p.102)

Linen Union GLASS CLOTH Linen Union

FOLD　　FOLD　　FOLD

Linen Union GLASS CLOTH Linen Union

Step 1

Unpick all the seams of the tea towel and press flat with a hot iron. Lay the towel horizontally in front of you and cut into three equal parts with two vertical cuts – each part will measure roughly 10 x 22in (25 x 56cm). Decorate your three pieces of fabric, filling the main white area in between the woven stripes. Create stripes and checks by machine in colour thread using straight stitch and small, close zigzag stitch (see stitch patterns, opposite). Finish off all the thread ends by hand – pull threads through to the wrong side, tie them off and trim to ¼in (5mm).

Step 2

Take one piece of fabric. Fold it in half wrong sides together and pin the sides so that the raw edges align. Draw a curve starting 3¼in (8cm) from each side of the two bottom corners – either draw freehand, or use a saucer or small plate as a guide. Cut along your drawn curves and then pin or tack around both sides. With white thread on your machine, stitch a ⅜in (1cm) seam around the two sides and along the bottom fold of your fabric. Remove any pins or tacking, trim the seam to ¼in (5mm) and turn wrong side out. Press the seams with a hot iron and pin or tack. Sew a ⅜in (1cm) seam around the sides and bottom of your bag to create a French seam. Remove any pins or tacking.

Step 3

Make three handles by taking 20in (50cm) of colour herringbone tape and folding it in half so it measures 10 x 1in (25 x 2.5cm). Machine ⅛in (3mm) in from both sides.

Step 4

With your bag still inside out, fold the top raw edge in ⅜in (1cm) and press. Pin either end of the handle to the centre point of the front and back top edge of your bag, overlapping the edge by ¾in (2cm). Take 20in (50cm) of the herringbone tape and align it with the folded top edge. Pin or tack it all the way round to cover the raw edge you have just folded over and the raw ends of the handle. Cut to length so that the two ends overlap by 1¼in (3cm). Tuck the last ⅜in (1cm) of the tape under and lay it over the beginning raw end of the tape to complete the circumference. Stitch around the top and bottom edges of the herringbone tape ⅛in (3mm) in. Remove any pins or tacking.

Step 5

Using a small, close zigzag stitch, stitch an 'X' at the base of the handle ends, giving them decorative extra strength.

See also:
Topstitching _page 105_
Zigzag stitch _page 105_
Trimming corners and curves _page 106_
French seams _page 107_

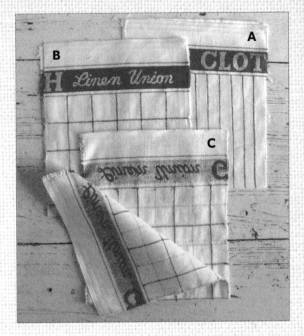

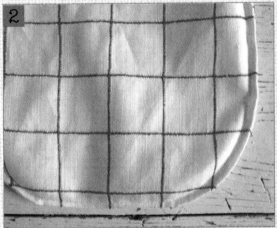

STITCH PATTERNS

A Small, close zigzag vertical lines ¾in (2cm) apart.

B Small, close zigzag vertical and horizontal lines 1½in (4cm) apart.

C Small, close zigzag vertical and horizontal lines 1½in (4cm) apart, alternated with vertical and horizontal lines of straight stitching centrally between the zigzag lines.

A fresh look at a familiar classic. Keep your teapot steaming hot with an (almost) plain quilted tea cosy. A sweet little rosette on either side adds a touch of decoration; you could add more to soften the simple silhouette. This cosy is lined with thermal wadding, making it extra efficient.

TEA COSY

Supplies:

(to fit teapot with 24 fluid oz/700ml capacity)

- ☐ 1 x tea towel, minimum dimensions 20 x 30in (50 x 76cm), or fabric of your choice cut to those measurements
- ☐ 24 x 16in (60 x 40cm) heatproof wadding*
- ☐ 65in (1.65m) of 1in (2.5cm) wide herringbone tape (or bias binding)*
- ☐ 2 x small white buttons
- ☐ 2 x small green buttons
- ☐ Sewing needle and pins

- ☐ White and green threads
- ☐ Sewing machine
- ☐ Scissors
- ☐ Iron
- ☐ Measuring tape

Stripe placement (see p.102)

* Amounts required will vary according to the size of your teapot.

MAKING A PAPER PATTERN

Use a tape to measure the circumference of your teapot. Make sure you measure the widest point, including the tip of the spout and the widest part of the handle. Now measure from the bottom of one side, over the tallest point and back down to the bottom of the other side. Add 2½in (6cm) to both your measurements, and then divide them by two. Draw up a rectangle using your calculations and round off the top left- and right-hand corners.

TEA COSY
Step 1

If you are using an Irish linen tea towel (if not, jump to step 3), cut along its length ⅜in (1cm) to the right of the left-hand thin stripes on each side.

Step 2

Align the two raw edges and sew a ⅜in (1cm) seam using the thin stripe as your guide. You now have a piece of linen with the stripe motif centred. Press the seam open ready to cut your pattern pieces.

Step 3

Cut your fabric and wadding using your paper pattern. Cut two pieces of linen, centring the stripe of your tea towel vertically, and cut two pieces of heatproof wadding. Pin each piece of wadding to the wrong side of the two pieces of linen.

Step 4

Score or mark vertical lines 1¼in (3cm) apart from the centre of the stripe out towards the sides.

Step 5

Working out from the centre, stitch the lines by machine, using thread to match your stripe for the central line and white thread thereafter. Once quilted, remove any pins or tacking. You may find that your piece needs trimming around the sides, as a certain amount of stretching can occur during the process. Zigzag all around by machine to minimize fraying. Repeat with the second side. Cut a piece of herringbone tape the length of the bottom of one of your quilted sides plus ¾in (2cm). Use it to bind the bottom edge.

Step 6

Trim any excess tape at either end so that it is flush with the sides and repeat with the other piece. Place both pieces wrong sides together. Pin or tack and machine stitch all the way around, ¼in (5mm) from the raw edges. Remove any pins or tacking. Cut a piece of herringbone tape that is long enough to cover the remaining curve from one side of your tea cosy to the other, plus ¾in (2cm). Fold the two raw ends under by ⅜in (1cm) and tack in place. Use it to bind the curved edge of your cosy. As you do so, insert one end of the herringbone loop under the tape at the centre of the top. Remove any pins or tacking.

Step 7

Turn the cosy over and sew the other side of the binding down by hand, tucking the other end of the herringbone loop under the tape at the top.

Step 8

Press with a hot iron. Secure the herringbone loop in position by stitching on two small white buttons, one on either side, with green thread.

Step 9

Make two rosettes from your linen scraps. Attach a rosette on either side, made from your linen scraps and secured with a small green button and white thread.

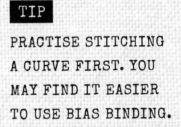

TIP

PRACTISE STITCHING
A CURVE FIRST. YOU
MAY FIND IT EASIER
TO USE BIAS BINDING.

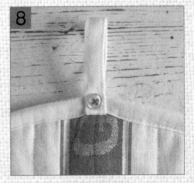

See also:

Topstitching *page 105*
Zigzag stitch *page 105*
Binding edges *page 110*
Making rosettes *page 115*

TECHNIQUES

MATERIALS AND EQUIPMENT

A sewing machine (see page 104) is essential for making the projects in this book. You will also need a steam iron and ironing board on hand to press your work as you go.

Other items you will need include: masking tape (1), embroidery threads (2), D-rings (3), fine knitting or crochet cotton (4), measuring tape (5), buttons (6), staple gun (7), safety pins (8), small brass curtain rings (9), pencil (10), seam ripper (stitch unpicker) (11), square-ended paintbrush (12), ruler (13), sewing shears (for fabric) (14), air-erasable pen (15), fabric paint (16), tea towels (17), T-shirt transfer paper (18), pins (19), threads (20), sewing and embroidery needles (21), bias binding (22), piping cord (23), rickrack (24), crochet hook (25), scissors (for paper) (26), small magnets (27), herringbone tape (28), zipper (29), ripstop fabric (30), heatproof cotton wadding (31) and fabric dye (32).

MODEL ARROW FASTENER CO. INC.
JT-21M SADDLE BROOK, N.J. U.S.A.

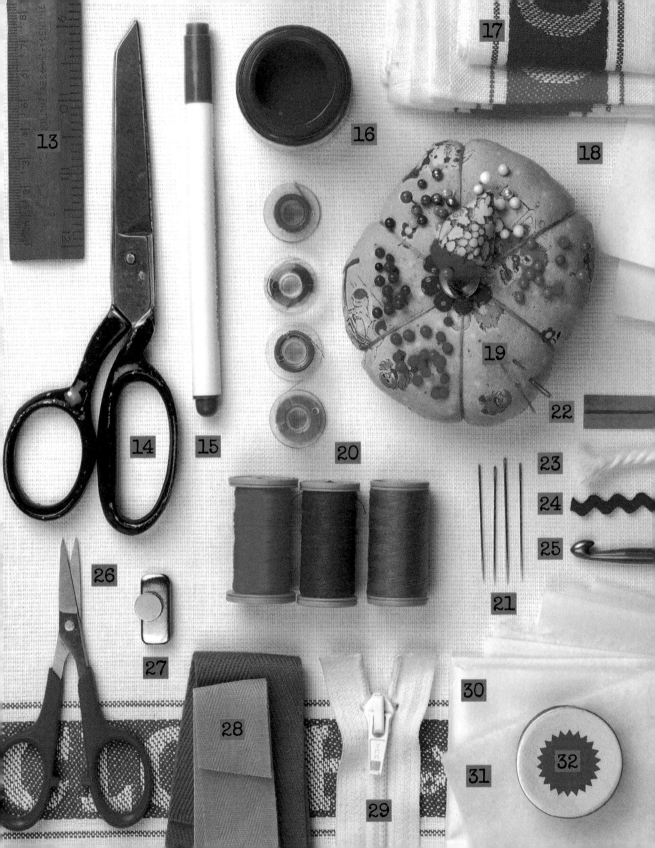

CHOOSING MATERIALS

Choose natural fibres whenever possible: linens, cottons or linen/cotton mixes. Natural fibres are best washed before use to pre-shrink. I have used ripstop fabric for a couple of projects, for its practicality and water resistance. It is best to avoid letting an iron have direct contact with ripstop. If it has heavy creases, leave it under a flat weight for a couple of days, or press under a cotton or linen cloth – check with the manufacturer.

For trims and ties use simple, traditional rickrack, piping cord, herringbone and woven tapes, 100% cotton threads and plain buttons.

STRIPE PLACEMENT

If you are using a patterned or striped tea towel for your project it's worth spending a bit of time planning the placement of the woven or printed design when cutting your fabric. The stripe placement diagrams throughout the book show you how I positioned the stripes in my projects.

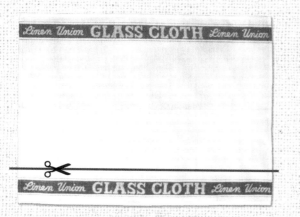

WORKING WITH FABRIC

MEASURING
A measuring tape can be substituted with a ruler. Whichever you use, make sure you consistently use either imperial or metric measurements and do not mix the two.

MARKING
You can use an air-erasable pen or a fabric marker. Most fade after a couple of hours, but do check as some need washing out. Tailor's chalk can be brushed away. Use white chalk on dark cloth and coloured chalk on lighter fabrics. The chalk should be kept sharp to produce a clean line. If your design is going to be stitched with a dark thread, you can simply use a very fine, sharp pencil to mark your fabric.

CUTTING
Ideally, you should have two pairs of sewing scissors. A small pair of sharp, pointed scissors is essential for cutting threads and trimming corners and curves. Sewing shears have long blades and a bent handle so that the scissors can rest on the table while cutting, keeping the fabric flat. Make sure your shears are used solely for fabrics and keep them sharp – it is a good idea to get them sharpened every couple of years.

> **TIP**
>
> I MARK THE HANDLES OF MY FABRIC SHEARS WITH A RIBBON SO THAT NO ONE USES THEM TO CUT PAPER.

PINNING AND TACKING (BASTING)
Pinning and tacking seams before you sew ensures that the fabric will not slip about when stitching, thereby producing a straight, neat seam. Pins with coloured glass heads are easy to find in fabric. Place your pins at right angles to your stitching line if you want to machine stitch over them and avoid having to tack or baste.

Tacking, also known as basting, is a temporary stitch used to fix pieces of fabric in position ready for permanent stitching. It is the easiest and quickest hand-sewing stitch. Knot the end of the thread and work large running stitches about ⅜in (1cm) long (**A**). Finish with a couple of stitches worked over each other to secure the end. When the seam or hem has been permanently sewn by machine, remove the tacking.

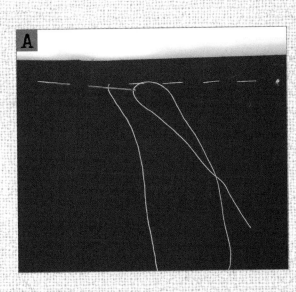

103

Techniques

USING A SEWING MACHINE

It is important to keep your sewing machine regularly serviced and covered when not in use. Always refer to your instruction booklet for information on threading, changing stitches, reversing, making buttonholes and so on.

A zipper sewing machine foot is an essential, as is a buttonhole foot, if you don't want to stitch these features by hand.

Set up your machine somewhere with plenty of light and where you can sit at the machine comfortably.

Before sewing, make sure that the machine is threaded correctly and that the threads from the needle and bobbin are placed away from you towards the back of the machine. Turn the wheel towards you so that the needle is in the work, preventing a tangle of threads as you start. Taking it slowly will ensure control of the machine and make problems with the tension or tangling threads less likely to arise.

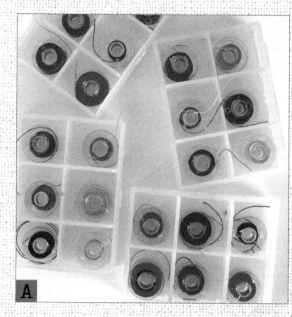

A

TWO-COLOUR SEWING

I regularly sew with one colour threaded on the machine needle and a different colour in the bobbin below. This is useful when sewing together two different coloured fabrics, making the stitching less visible on both sides. I keep little pill boxes of fully charged bobbins in all the colours I'll be using in projects (A), so that I can swap the bobbin over quickly when I need to.

When using this technique it is especially important that your stitch tension is even so that the alternative colours are not pulled through to show on the other side of your fabric.

TIP

IT IS A GOOD IDEA TO KEEP SCRAPS OF THE FABRIC YOU ARE WORKING WITH TO TEST OUT YOUR MACHINE STITCH SIZE AND TENSION BEFORE STARTING ON YOUR PROJECT.

BASIC STITCHES

I don't go in for fancy sewing-machine stitching: the basics of straight stitching, zigzag stitching, reverse stitching and buttonholes are all you need to make the projects in this book.

STRAIGHT STITCH (A)
Used for all flat seams, hems and topstitching. You can alter the length of straight stitch – at its longest it can be used for gathering or tacking (basting).

TOPSTITCHING (B)
A line of straight machine stitching worked on the right side of the fabric, parallel to seams and edges. It can be used as both a decorative and a functional stitch, providing extra strength to a hem or seam.

ZIGZAG STITCH (C)
Used along raw edges to help reduce fraying. Zigzag stitches can also be used decoratively or to strengthen pressure or stress points. You can alter the length of the stitches and how close together they are. When changing from straight stitch to zigzag (or vice versa) without breaking your stitching, always adjust your stitch function with the foot down (to hold your fabric in position) and the needle up.

REVERSE STITCHING (D)
This reinforces or strengthens the beginning and end of a line of stitching, particularly in areas where pressure or stress will occur. It can also be used as a quick way to start and end stitching without having to finish off thread ends by hand.

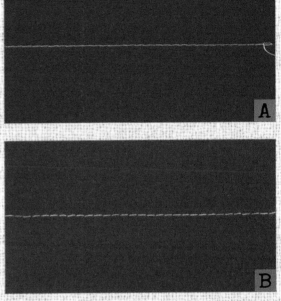

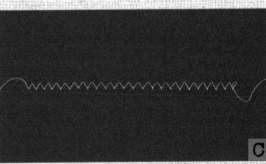

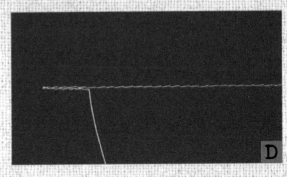

BASIC SEAMS

FLAT SEAMS (A)
Place the two pieces of fabric together, right sides facing. Pin or tack the fabric together. Machine stitch along your sewing line, ⅜in (1cm) from, and parallel to, the raw edges of the fabrics. Finish the beginning and end of your line of stitching either by hand or by reverse stitching.

FINISHING OFF THREADS (B)
Finish off thread ends by threading them onto a sewing needle and either making a couple of small, tight stitches before cutting the thread off, or 'losing' the ends into a French seam or hem.

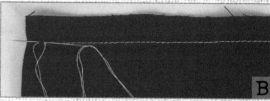

TRIMMING CORNERS AND CURVES (C)
Corners should be trimmed to an angle of 90° so they are sharp when the work is turned right side out. On curved seams, cut V-shapes into the seam close to the stitch line. This will allow the seam to be smooth when the work is turned right side out.

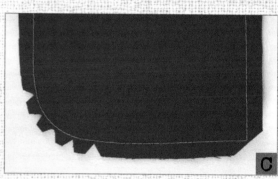

PRESSING SEAMS (D)
Have all the equipment for ironing set up before you start a project. Press each seam as you complete it. Use the point of the iron to open seams and steam for a crisp edge and a flat seam.

UNPICKING SEAMS (E)
A seam ripper (or stitch unpicker) is a useful tool used for unpicking stitches. Insert the pointed blade underneath the thread to be cut. Push it forwards against the thread and the blade will cut it. It is possible to run the blade along a line of stitching between the two layers of fabric and cut all the stitches in one movement, but this requires some skill and can end in tears.

FRENCH SEAMS

Step 1
With the right sides of your fabric together, align your raw hem edges. Pin or tack together and stitch a ⅜in (1cm) seam along the edge.

Step 2
Trim the seam to ¼in (5mm).

Step 3
Turn wrong side out and press with an iron. Pin or tack all the way along the seam and stitch a ⅜in (1cm) hem, thus encasing the raw edges. Finally, turn right side out and press.

TIP

FRENCH SEAMS ARE AN EFFICIENT WAY TO PREVENT RAW EDGES FRAYING. THE SEAM COMPLETELY ENCASES THE EDGES LEAVING A NEAT FINISH. THEY ARE IDEAL FOR ITEMS THAT WILL GET A LOT OF WEAR.

MAKING BOX CORNERS

Step 1

Place the two pieces of fabric right sides together. Using a straight stitch, and the indicated seam allowance, sew the side and bottom seams. Pivot at the corners by leaving the needle down, raising the foot and turning the fabric 90°.

Step 2

Press the seams open. With the sewn fabric still right sides together, match the side seam with the bottom fold (or seam) to create a point at the corner. Pin to hold them together. It is very important that you exactly match the seams; this will make your finished corner look good.

Step 3

Mark the line of the box corner with a pencil so the depth is measured from side to side at the base of the point. This boxed corner depth is 4in (10cm), measured from the tip of the corner.

Step 4

Sew across the point on the drawn line several times, reverse stitching at the beginning and end for extra strength.

Step 5

Trim away the peak to ¼in (5mm) from the line of stitching.

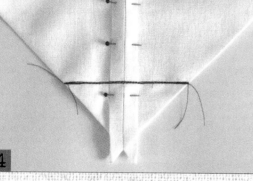

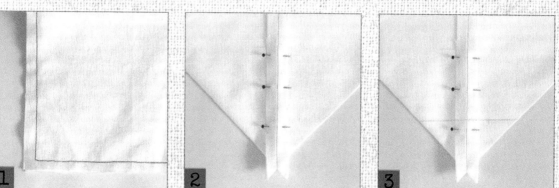

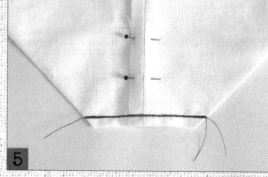

INSERTING A ZIPPER

Step 1

Place your two pieces of fabric right sides together and with the raw edges aligned where you want your zipper positioned. Place your zipper in position along this edge and mark the position of either end of the teeth with a pin. Remove the zipper and pin or tack along the seam, retaining the two marking pins. Stitch a ⅜in (1cm) seam in from either end up to the zipper marking pins, reversing at both these points for extra strength. Now change your machine to a long stitch and sew a ⅜in (1cm) seam between the two markers.

Step 2

Open out the fabric and press the seam open. With the fabric right side down, lay the zipper face down on top centred between the markers. Pin or tack all the way around.

Step 3

Turn the fabric over and sew in the zipper using a zipper foot or a piping foot on your machine. Finally, use a seam ripper to remove the long seam stitches between the two markers.

TIP

ZIPPERS WITH METAL TEETH MUST BE THE CORRECT LENGTH — PLASTIC ONES CAN BE TRIMMED TO FIT (AT THE BOTTOM, FIXED END).

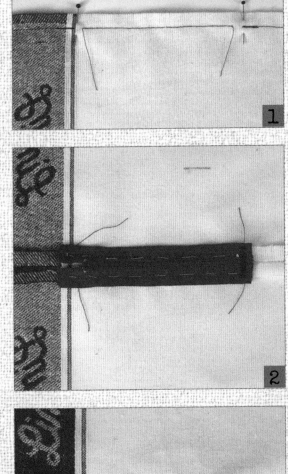

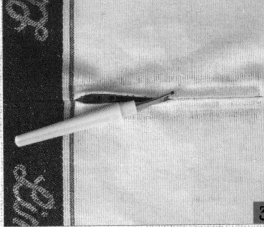

BINDING EDGES

Use tape, bias binding or strips of fabric to bind raw edges. If you are making your own binding from strips of fabric, cut them wider than needed, fold the long edges in and press them before starting.

Step 1

Cut your binding to the required length plus at least ¾in (2cm). Lay the binding along the edge of your work so that the middle of the binding lies exactly over the raw fabric edge. Pin or tack in position and topstitch along the binding ⅛in (3mm) or less from the edge. If binding all the way around a piece of work, join it by folding the end under ⅜in (1cm), overlapping the beginning of the binding and stitching along this fold.

Step 2

Turn your work over. Fold the tape down to meet the stitch line and encase the raw edges. Hem by hand with overstitch.

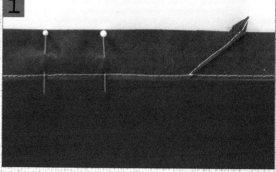

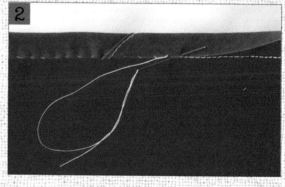

BINDING AROUND CURVES

Any curved edges require fabric cut on the bias to avoid excessive puckering. The easiest way to do this is to use pre-made bias binding.

Step 1

Open the binding out. Place it on your work right sides together and position the upper fold in the binding along your stitch line. Tack in place and machine slowly and carefully along the fold crease.

Step 2

Fold the binding over the raw edges of your work to the other side. Fold the binding under and hem by hand with overstitch. Press on both sides.

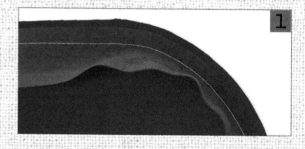

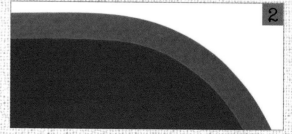

BINDING A MITRED CORNER

Mitred corners are crisp and sharp, and well worth the effort for binding tablecloths and quilts. Use binding that measures twice the width you want it to finish up; so for a ½in (1.25cm) bound border use 1in (2.5cm) wide strips of binding.

Step 1

You need enough binding to cover your seams, plus 3in (7cm) for finishing off. Measure the width of your binding. Draw a line half the width of your binding in from the raw edges to be bound. Starting halfway along one edge, lay your binding right side up so that its bottom edge lies on your pencil line. Topstitch by machine very close to the bottom edge of the binding until you reach the corner turn of the pencil line. Remove your work from the machine and finish off the thread ends by hand.

Step 2

Fold your binding back under itself and upwards at an angle of 90°.

Step 3

Now fold the binding back down under itself again 180° so that the mitre's point lies exactly over the corner point of the fabric.

Step 4

Re-insert the machine needle where your last stitching finished, in the corner fold – turn the wheel by hand to place it accurately – and topstitch close to the edge of the binding along the edge of your work to the next corner.

Step 5

Turn your work over. Fold the binding down to encase the raw seam edge. Pin or tack in position before hemming all the way around by hand using overstitch. Take your time at the corners to fold neat mitres to mirror those on the other side.

Step 6

Press the binding from both sides to neaten any 'wonky' corners.

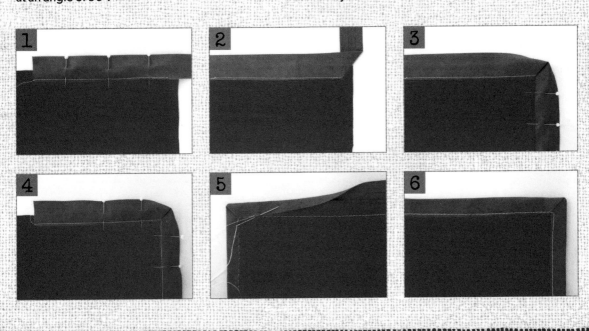

HAND FINISHING STITCHES

OVERSTITCH (A)
Use overstitch for closing openings left for turning. With your two pieces of fabric pinned or tacked together, bring your needle up from within one folded edge to the front of your work. Now push your needle diagonally through both folded layers, catching a few threads of fabric from each. Pull the needle and thread through and repeat, spacing your stitches between ⅛in (3mm) and ¼in (5mm) apart.

HEM STITCH (B)
Similar to overstitch, this stitch is used for hand stitching hems.

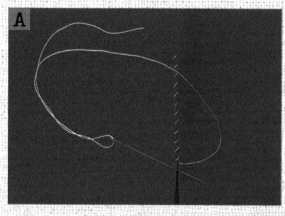

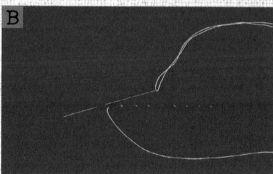

SEWING ON BUTTONS

Mark the position for your button on the fabric. With your thread doubled, tie a knot at the end and pull your needle through to the front of your fabric. Sew the button on securely through the holes, then pull the needle through between the button and the fabric. Wind the thread around the stitches connecting the button to the fabric twice. Insert the needle through to the back of the fabric and finish off with a couple of small, tight stitches.

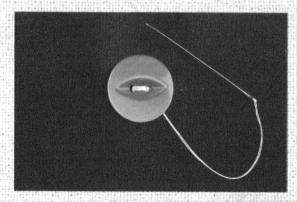

MAKING BUTTONHOLES

For horizontal buttonholes, the position of the button should be near the end closest to the opening. For vertical buttonholes, the position of the button should be central.

Step 1

Measure your button diameter – this will be the length of your buttonhole. Use a sharp pencil to draw a line which is the correct measurement for your buttonhole. Cut along the line with small, sharp scissors.

Step 2

Sew small running stitches around the circumference of your buttonhole (or sew overstitches if the fabric frays easily).

Step 3

Starting at one end of the buttonhole, make very close buttonhole stitches (blanket stitch; see embroidery stitches on page 117) all around the opening, about ⅛in (3mm) long.

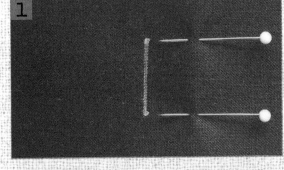

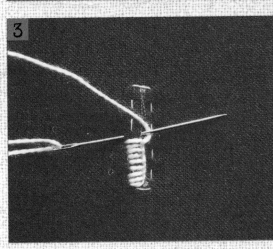

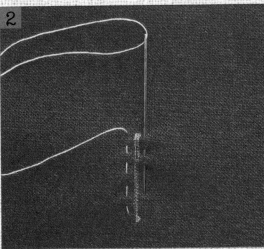

TIP

IF YOU HAVE MADE YOUR BUTTONHOLE A LITTLE TOO BIG, YOU CAN REDUCE IT SLIGHTLY BY CLOSING IT UP AT ONE END WITH A FEW SMALL, TIGHT STITCHES.

MAKING DRAWSTRING TABS

Step 1

Cut a rectangle of linen 2½ x 6¼in (6.5 x 16cm).
Lay it down vertically in front of you right side up.
Fold the short top edge back ⅜in (1cm) and press.
Place the two piping cord ends on top, running
down the centre and ending 2¼in (6cm) below the
bottom edge. Stitch by machine back and forth
across the cord a few times ⅛in (3mm) above the
bottom edge.

Step 2

Fold the short bottom edge of the fabric up to meet
the top edge (right sides facing). At the same time,
fold the bottom edge over ⅜in (1cm) along the
stitch line so that the majority of the piping cord
is still above the tab and the raw ends are lying
vertically down the centre of the fabric, aligning
with the bottom edge. Pin or tack and machine
stitch a ⅜in (1cm) seam down both sides.

Step 3

Trim all four corners at 90° and turn right side out.
Tease the corners to make them sharp. Press, then
stitch back and forth several times across the top
edge close to the tab to firmly secure the cord.

MAKING ROSETTES

Step 1

Cut a 9¾ x 1¾in (25 x 4.5cm) strip of linen. With the wrong side facing, fold both long edges of the strip over ⅜in (1cm) and press. Pin or tack and stitch along it with a large zigzag stitch.

> **TIP**
>
> USE DIFFERENT AREAS OF PATTERN AND COLOUR FROM YOUR SCRAPS OF TEA TOWEL TO CREATE VARIED FLOWER STYLES.

Step 2

Fold in half, right sides together, pin or tack and stitch the two short ends together with a ⅜in (1cm) seam in straight stitch, then zigzag the raw ends to minimize fraying.

Step 3

Turn right side out. Make long running stitches by hand ⅛in (3mm) in from one long folded edge of your 'ring' of fabric with your thread doubled. Pull the thread tight to gather (with the needle still attached) and make several stitches on the wrong side to retain the gathering.

EMBROIDERY

Embellishing your work with embroidery adds a very personal touch. These five simple stitches can be used in different sizes and combinations to create numerous decorative images and textures.

Don't be tempted to use more than 18in (45cm) of embroidery thread at a time. If you do, it will most likely get twisted and knotted while you work.

As you become more skilled, take time to study your pattern and plan your 'route' around it – one that causes as little crisscrossing across the back of your work as possible. You should try to keep the reverse neat if you can.

If you are new to embroidery, using a fabric with a clearly visible weave, such as linen, helps keep you on course if you're working on a geometric design.

Finish your threads by weaving them in and out along a line of stitching at the reverse on your work for ⅜in (1cm) or so before trimming the thread.

Use the right type of needle for embroidery. Sharps have a relatively large eye, making them fairly easy to thread for hand stitching. Embroidery needles are thicker and have a larger eye to accommodate the thicker embroidery thread.

COUCHING STITCH

Step 1
Couching stitch is made with either one or two threads – using two allows you to play with colours. With one thread, make a long straight stitch – 2in (5cm) or more. With a second thread, bring the thread out to the front of your fabric to one side and up close to your long stitch and ⅛in (3mm) from its beginning. Make a small stitch inserting the needle on the other side of the long stitch, thus holding it in place.

Step 2
Bring the needle out to the front about ⅜in (1cm) further along the long stitch. Continue making small stitches along its length, anchoring it to the fabric. Continue until the whole long stitch is anchored.

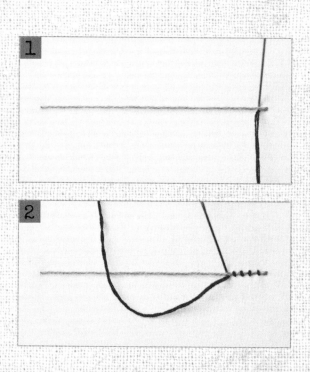

BACKSTITCH

Step 1

Use backstitch to outline shapes to fill with more decorative stitching. Bring the thread through to the front of your fabric on your stitch line. Make a small running stitch, about ¼in (5mm) long, along the stitch line, bringing the needle back through to the front again, ¼in (5mm) from your first stitch.

Step 2

Reinsert the needle ¼in (5mm) back along the stitch line at the point where your last stitch went through to the back of your work. Pull the needle through to the front again, ¼in (5mm) ahead of the last stitch. Continue, creating a solid line of ¼in (5mm) stitches.

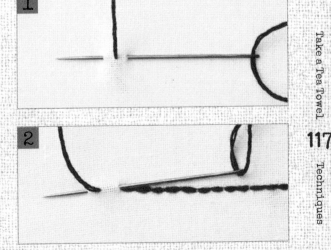

BLANKET STITCH

Step 1

Imagine two parallel stitch lines roughly ¼in (5mm) apart. Bring your thread through to the front of your work on the left-hand line. Insert the needle in position ¼in (5mm) further along in the right-hand line and through to the front again parallel to where it was inserted, at the same time keeping the working thread under the needle point (1a). Pull your thread through and to the left to form an L-shape (1b).

Step 2

Reinsert the needle ¼in (5mm) further along in the right-hand line and through to the front again parallel to where it was inserted before, at the same time keeping the working thread under the needle point. Continue, creating an even line of stitches.

CHAIN STITCH

Use chain stitch for bolder outlines, or use individual chains for petal and seed shapes (once your stitch is complete, insert the needle through to the back of your work on the other side of the working thread to anchor it).

Step 1

Bring the thread through to the front of your fabric on your stitch line and hold it down with the left thumb. Insert the needle where it emerged from and bring the needle out ¼in (5mm) further along the stitch line, keeping the working thread under the needle's point as you do so.

Step 2

Pull the thread through, thus trapping a loop of your thread to produce the 'chain'.

Step 3

Repeat steps 1 and 2 to your last stitch.

Step 4

End by inserting the needle through to the back of your work on the other side of the working thread to anchor it (4a and 4b).

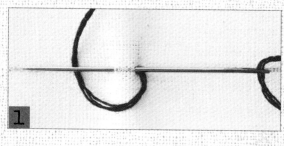

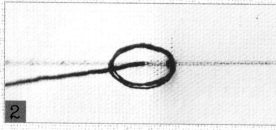

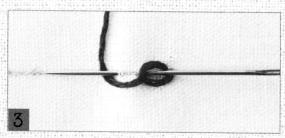

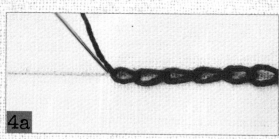

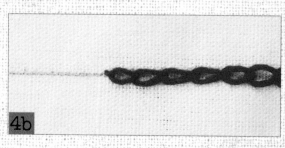

TIP

THE INSTRUCTIONS GIVEN HERE ARE FOR RIGHT-HANDERS. IF YOU ARE LEFT-HANDED, TRANSPOSE ALL LEFT/RIGHT INSTRUCTIONS.

FRENCH KNOTS

Step 1

Bring the thread out to the front of your fabric.
With your left thumb, hold the thread down where it
emerges, then with your right hand wrap the thread
three times around the needle's point.

> **TIP**
>
> MAKE YOUR KNOTS BIGGER OR
> SMALLER BY WRAPPING YOUR THREAD
> AROUND THE NEEDLE FROM TWO TO
> SIX TIMES (MORE THAN THIS IS
> LIKELY TO GET YOU IN A TANGLE!).

Step 2

Slide your 'wraps' of thread down to the eye of the
needle and hold them in place with your thumbnail.

Step 3

Pull your needle and thread through the tight
wraps, sliding them down to the fabric surface.

Step 4

Insert the needle back through close to where the
thread first emerged (not in the exact same place
or it will simply pull back through). Pull the needle
through to the back, leaving a knot on the surface.

> **TIP**
>
> VERY TIGHTLY CLUSTERED
> FRENCH KNOTS CAN CREATE
> A RAISED TEXTURE.

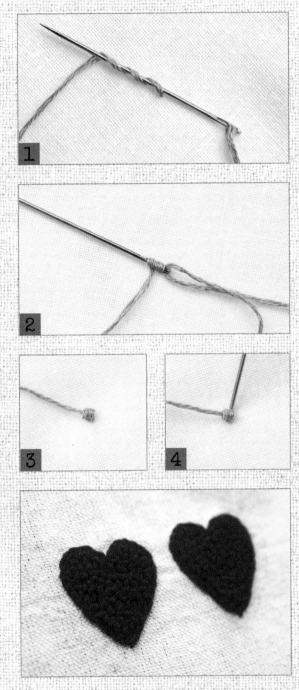

FABRIC PAINTING

Step 1

Draw your design freehand onto your fabric using either a sharp, fine pencil or an air-erasable pen. Alternatively, trace your design onto your fabric using a lightbox or by taping the design to a windowpane and holding the fabric up against it.

Step 2

Mix your fabric paints to the colour you want. Turn your fabric as you work so that you minimize the risk of smudging. When you are painting your fabric, try to keep the paint even and smooth – lumps will potentially chip off later, leaving a white blemish.

When you have finished painting, leave the piece to dry and then set it by ironing (always follow the manufacturer's instructions).

TIP

A LIGHTBOX IS A SHALLOW BOX CONTAINING AN ELECTRIC LIGHT BULB, WITH A TOP SURFACE OF TRANSLUCENT GLASS OR PLASTIC. IT IS PERFECT FOR TRACING MOTIFS AND DESIGNS ON TO LIGHT FABRICS.

TIP

USING A SQUARE-HEADED BRUSH WILL HELP YOU TO ACHIEVE SHARP, STRAIGHT EDGES ON YOUR DESIGN.

IRON-ON TRANSFERS

Step 1
Print your photograph or images onto an A4 sheet of T-shirt transfer paper with either a photocopier or a printer. Trim to about ¼in (5mm) around your image with sharp paper scissors.

Step 2
Iron onto your fabric following the instructions on the transfer packaging. Check by carefully lifting a corner of the backing paper to see if the heat of the iron has done its job, and that the image is firmly adhering to the fabric.

Step 3
Gently peel the backing paper away.

TIP

ALWAYS PROTECT YOUR TRANSFER FROM DIRECT HEAT — FOLLOW THE MANUFACTURER'S INSTRUCTIONS.

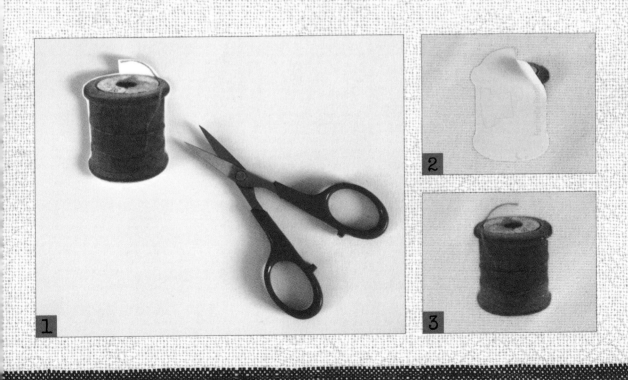

1

2

3

Templates

All the templates you need for embroidering, painting and printing on your projects are here. But be inspired: take your own photographs for your sewing-machine cover, embroider Victorian dolly pegs on your clothes-peg bag or a sailor's knot on your string holder.

They can all be photocopied at 100% apart from the Linen Bag symbols on page 123, which should be enlarged to 150% size.

Sewing-machine Cover p.32

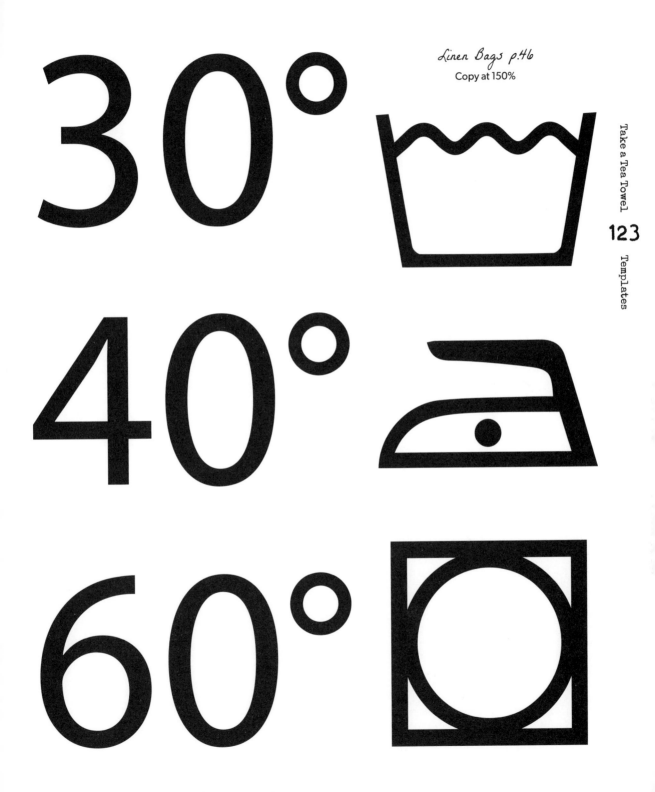

30°

Linen Bags p.46
Copy at 150%

40°

60°

String Holder p.36
Cut out around red line

5·75 – 6·0   10

5·25 – 5·5   9

4·75 – 5·0   8

4·25 – 4·5   7

3·75 – 4·0   6

3·25 – 3·5   5

2·75 – 3·0   4

2·25 – 2·5   3

Knitting-needle Roll p.40

Bedlinen Envelopes p.50

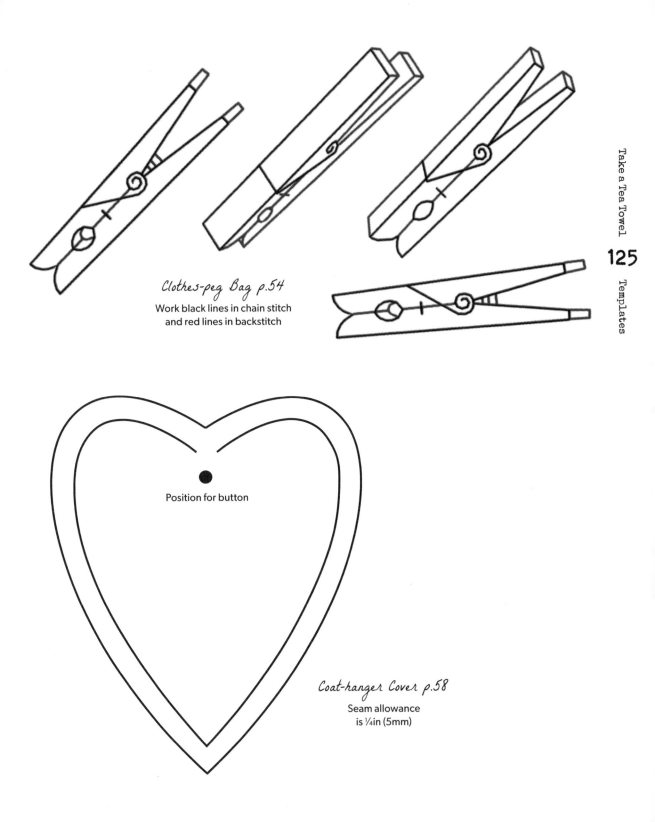

Clothes-peg Bag p.54

Work black lines in chain stitch
and red lines in backstitch

Position for button

Coat-hanger Cover p.58

Seam allowance
is ¼in (5mm)

Suppliers

ART SUPPLIES
Clarkes Office Supplies
www.clarkesofficesupplies.co.uk
106–108 South Road,
Haywards Heath, West Sussex,
RH16 4LL, UK

LINEN UNION GLASS CLOTHS
TTB Supplies
www.ttbsupplies.com
Unit 16, Highgrove Farm
Industrial Estate, Seaford,
Pinvin, Worcestershire,
WR10 2LF, UK

The Linen House
www.linenhouse.co.uk
10 Station Road West,
Oxted, Surrey, RH8 9EP, UK

PHOTO TRANSFER PAPER
Avery
www.avery.co.uk
5 The Switchback,
Gardner Road, Maidenhead,
Berkshire, SL6 7RJ, UK

RIPSTOP FABRIC
GoKites
www.gokites.co.uk
4 Riverside Workshops,
Coniston Road, Blyth Riverside
Business Park, Blyth,
Northumberland, NE24 4RF, UK

THREADS, BUTTONS,
TRIMS AND TAPES
The Brighton Sewing Centre
www.brightonsewingcentre.
co.uk
68 North Road, Brighton,
East Sussex, BN1 1YD, UK

C & H Fabrics
www.candh.co.uk
Stone House,
21/23 Church Road, Tunbridge
Wells, Kent, TN1 1HT, UK

John Lewis Partnership
www.johnlewis.com
PO Box 19615, Erskine,
PA8 6WU, UK

Acknowledgements

AUTHOR'S ACKNOWLEDGEMENTS A huge thank you to Jonathan, Gilda, Virginia and everyone at GMC who helped in the production of this book and Holly J for the great photographs. To Emma K for encouraging me in the first place. There are too many others – good friends – to name individually for fear of missing anyone out... and, of course, my lovely family. Thank you x

GMC PUBLICATIONS would like to thank: Ruth Crimes and Dodo House, West Wittering, West Sussex, UK, for allowing us to photograph in their beautiful beach house, Emma Foster for planning and assisting at the photo shoot, The White Company, The Patchwork Dog & Basket in Lewes, and Martha Bamford for the loan of props, and Ben and Guy for helping us to move everything.

Index

Page numbers in bold contain photographs of the completed projects.

To place an order, or to request a catalogue, contact:

GMC Publications Ltd, Castle Place, 166 High Street, Lewes, East Sussex, BN7 1XU, United Kingdom

Tel: +44 (0)1273 488005
www.gmcbooks.com